RITUAL ART OF INDIA

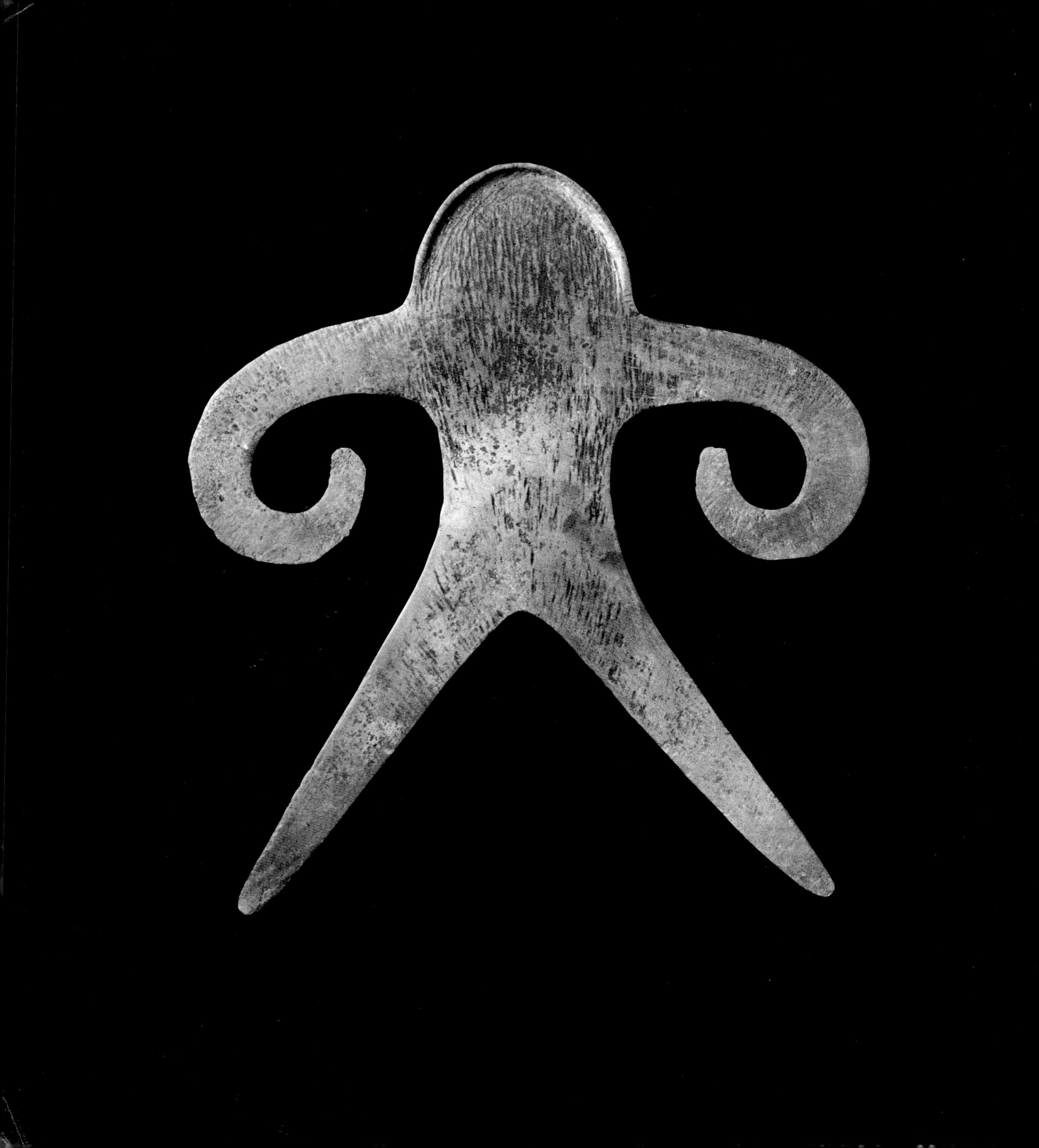

RITUAL ART OF INDIA

AJIT MOOKERJEE

with 135 illustrations
101 in colour

THAMES AND HUDSON

To Dr Maurie D. Pressman, in gratitude

FRONTISPIECE
1 Cosmic Man. Ritual figure from the Bissauli 'copper hoards', *c.*1000 BC.

First paperback edition 1998

British Library Cataloguing-in-Publication Data
A catalogue record for this book is available from the British Library

ISBN 0-500-28058-4

Printed and bound in Hong Kong by Dai Nippon

CONTENTS

ॐ अखण्डमण्डलाकारं व्याप्तं येन चराचरम् ।
तत्पदं दर्शितं येन तस्मै श्रीगुरवे नमः ॥८५॥

OṂ

All the animate and inanimate beings that comprise
the universe, which has the form of an unbroken circle,
are permeated by Brahman who is beyond these.
I bow to that supreme reality.

Skanda Purāṇa

PREFACE

As the twentieth century draws towards its close, the striving for spiritual perspective is forcing us to look inwards and question how we may realize our fullest spiritual potential. This study is an attempt to reveal the inward-seeking quality of Indian art, no matter what its subject-matter, iconography or chronology. The attunement of perception through the sensibilities which it provides is one of the reasons why it has been seen as a *mārga*, or way.

In the quest for spiritual identity one goes through constant transformations to discover a truth which is based on direct experience. Though the paths are many, the direction of all is the same. In its creative freedom, the ritual art of India has a vital message.

I am grateful to Dr Maurie D. Pressman, Clearwater, and Dr Cecil E. Burney, San Diego, for their help and encouragement; to Madhu Khanna, in particular, for her various helpful comments and information; to Priya Mookerjee, Mangla Sharda, and also Madhu Khanna, for providing me with special photographs; and to Pria Devi for her co-operation.

A.M.

I used to worship the Deity in the Kālī Temple. It was suddenly revealed to me that everything is Pure Spirit. The utensils of worship, the altar, the door frame – all Pure Spirit. Men, animals, and other living beings – all Pure Spirit. Then like a madman I began to shower flowers in all directions. Whatever I saw I worshipped.

RAMAKRISHNA

Introduction

$E = mc^2$

Einstein's equation tells us that matter is energy, and energy, matter. In the past, matter was conceived of as something entirely separate from a state of consciousness; but now, with a paradigmatic shift in understanding, we grasp that when matter and spirit are fused, the ultimate reality of life is revealed.

Ritual art is a means or way towards spiritual identity, towards a state in which we can realize our oneness with the universe. This realization is not something that descends from above; rather, it is an illumination to be discovered within. The unity underlying the diversity of the world is to be discovered in our relationship with all life, manifest and non-manifest. Integration of the self is achieved in ritual worship which opens up contact with each and every atom of our being. Ritual works on the assumption that nothing, however small and apparently insignificant, or vast and incomprehensible, is without significance to our destiny in this *jagat*, the ever-moving world.

Traditionally, Indian ritual art is a way of sharing *sādhanā*, one's progressive unification with the vital principle. Whereas Western religious art has tended to deal with answers that have been institutionally established, Indian ritual art draws the maker or viewer into a relationship. It is an experience, daily repeated, which leads towards integration, and to an expansion of consciousness which gives rise to perception of the whole.

The arts have their origin in ritual. Whether to invoke and propitiate deities, exorcise negative forces, to celebrate rites of passage or mark turning points in the cycle of death and renewal, ritual creates a focus and compacts energy. From incantation comes gesture; from gesture, the objects and utensils used for offerings. Their forms and arrangements create the ritual aesthetic. The orientation of sacred space requires the temple and the yantra; the point of focus, the abstract symbol or icon representing divine power.

Ritual art assembles and disposes the various objects of our awareness in a pattern of offering. Each thing to be offered must be the purest and finest of its kind – the dawn-flower, its perfume whole, blood-red mercuric oxide, chalk-white camphor, cool sandalwood paste, grain and herbs according to the season, and to the season in the cyclical life of the deity. The object is to create beauty and harmony, but more, to entrap and concentrate power for the benefit of celebrant and community.

How a society perceives the continual process of cultural interaction determines its unique value system. The Indian tradition has been receptive to new elements, and over time, has generated an entire range of philosophic and mystical approaches to the problems of existence. It has assimilated into itself innumerable cults, sects and ways of thinking – some more obviously radical in their approach, or confrontation with reality, others more classical. This dynamic outlook has prevented cultural breakdown or the disintegration and extinction of the civilization. The incoming elements are absorbed into the old cultural pattern, and the old is widened in fresh and often striking ways, to meet the needs of every type of person, facing every sort of question, at different ages and in different environments. Whenever any influence came its way, the blend of cultural forces assimilated as much of it as was in harmony with itself without losing its own basic character.

The central, unifying feature of all Indian spiritual life is *kriyā*, the timely fulfillment of ritual performance. *Kriyā* means 'action', and it is according to the principles of right action that life runs its course. All the rhythms of nature have their counterpart in the progressions of human life. The ritual act is right performance; the creation of a work of art likewise. Ritual asserts the Indian sense of human community, and of collaboration with the creative rhythms of the world.

The wisdom of 'right action' is the wisdom of retaining equilibrium in a condition of change. The *Bhagavadgītā* was the first text to describe how this equilibrium is to be preserved. Right action is disinterested; the only motive is self-alignment and cultivation of the sense of perfection.

The history of Indian ritual begins with the Vedic period (*c.* 1500 BC). The Vedic tradition of the fire altar (*yajña*) is known to us. It begins with
15 the establishing of the centre and the orientation of sacred space. The
12 building of the fire altar of bricks, the timing of the rites, the ceremonies
14 of the kindling of the sacred light and the pouring of libations, the mythology that gives the ritual its numerous dimensions of meaning – all have their source at the time of the world's oldest literature, the *Ṛig Veda*.

Ritual and mythology were amplified at the period of the *Brāhmaṇas* (*c.* 900–700 BC). These are texts in which various groups of sages supply commentaries on the Vedic hymns, describing and schematizing the sacrificial ceremonies and recording the histories and meanings of the observances. More philosophical and innovative are the *Upanishads*, a series of post-Vedic works embodying the mystical and esoteric doctrines of ancient Hindu philosophy. The fundamental doctrine of the *Upanishads* is the identity of the individual soul, Ātman, and the Universal Soul, Brahman.

Gradually during the post-Vedic period reform movements emerged, advocating the ascetic path to personal liberation. Alongside these movements are the texts of the 'six views' (*shaḍ darśana*) of classical Hindu philosophy. The last of these, the *Mīmāṁsā*, while directing attention to Vedic thought, reformulates the meaning of the fire sacrifice in metaphysical terms. It is the reflection of a growing spirit of rational enquiry, and its emergence is a sign that the way of personal ascetism was not to be the way for all. The *Gṛihya-sūtras* and the *Saṁhitās* (ritual handbooks) are the earliest texts concerned with domestic ritual observance. The rites they set out are fairly simple, some prescribed to be performed regularly, some on important occasions. In addition, the texts give rules for the religious conduct of the household, typically specifying rites marking the different stages of life. The massive public *yajña*-of-power began slowly to recede, leaving behind only its powerful hymns.

The early sacrificial implements and objects so far excavated are found to be simple but specialized. They include a great number of cups, pots, bowls, ladles and sieves, made of metal, stone, clay or wood. Nude female figurines, such as that dated 800 BC from the burial mounds at Lauriya-Nandangaḍh, recall the Earth Goddess of the Vedic burial hymns. The most striking metal ritual figure is that dated *c.*1000 from the Bissauli copper hoards, an abstract representation that seems to *1*
anticipate the Jain depictions of 'man as universe', or Cosmic Man, the Perfected One epitomizing the whole cosmos. The *Ṛig Veda* contains a famous reference (in the *Purusha-sūkta*) to the sacrifice of 'Purusha', man, representing the primal male or Male Principle. Sāṁkhya, one of the oldest systems of Hindu philosophy (*c.* 500 BC) identifies the two ultimate realities as Purusha, Cosmic Spirit, Unborn Male, and Prakṛiti, Cosmic Substance including matter, Unborn Female. Everything is held to be potential in these two ultimate 'uncaused' realities.

In the *Āgamas* (a class of instructional dialogue included among the *Tantras*, such as the *Śaiva Āgama*, in which Śiva addresses his consort Pārvatī), the Cosmic Being is Śiva, male, and the Creative Energy, Śakti, female.

Some Tantric rituals emphasize the worship of Śakti, the Creative Energy of Śiva, since she projects the divine bi-unity of masculine and feminine principles. In the Sāṁkhya system Prakṛiti is the prime mover, womb of the recurring cycles of the universe.

Purusha and Prakṛiti, Śiva and Śakti, though distinct in qualities, are inseparable, since they are essentially two aspects of one principle. The whole universe and manifold experience are Purusha-Prakṛiti, or Śiva-Śakti. The aim of ritual and active contemplation is to accomplish within oneself the integration of these polarities.

Buddhism (500 BC) and Jainism were additions to the Indian mainstream, and particularly in the case of Buddhism, contributed substantially to both philosophy and ritual. Tantra evolved its own rituals and became widespread. Local indigenous cults with a symbolism and ritual practice of their own continued as living tradition, incorporating much derived from the Vedic period.

The distinctions between the rituals associated with each of these systems are not as absolute as would first appear. Common to all is the view of ritual as reverence and preparation of the spirit, and as a stairway leading from the outer reality to the inner, from the immediate and perceptible to the transcendental plane.

From the celebration of the household fires to the marriage ceremony and the rites of the cremation ground, every stage of human life is marked by rituals which become a part of individual awareness. Right performance is learned at the feet of the guru when the child is initiated into the community of *dvi-jas*, 'twice-born', born-of-the-womb and born-of-ritual. Daily rites include the greeting of the sun at its rising – a cycle of yogic and ritual gestures directed towards the east and accompanied by prescribed mantras – the offering of grain and clarified butter to the pure flame, and the *saṅdhyā* or twilight prayers, recited as dusk falls when lamps are lighted in every traditional home to the sound of bell and gong.

There are rites for marriage, for consecration of the womb; for birth, for naming of the child, for carrying it out for the first time to face the rising sun, for the child's first feeding with solid food, for the shaving of its head, and for education, including investiture with the sacred thread, and rites for the completion of studies. According to the *varṇāśrama* system, a man relinquishes his responsibilities for family ritual observances only when he withdraws into *sannyāsa*, the renunciation of worldly desires. At his death, his sons will perform the rites of the pyre, and his spirit will be remembered with elaborate ceremonies for the ancestors, or those who have preceded us into death.

The techniques of meditation similarly include ritual. There are ritual gestures of the hands (*mudrās*), bodily stances and postures (*āsanas*); and the choice of timing and the whole preparation of the environment for meditation are ritually determined.

Seasonal festivals, pilgrimages, dedications of temple icons, indeed all the events, great and small, of personal and community life are accompanied by appropriate rites.

Ritual practices are of several kinds. *Bāhyapūjā* is object- or image-worship, and gives way to *mānasa-pujā*, mental reverence; and so to *parā-pūjā*, or transcendental worship. Devotion to one's *ishṭa*, the form or appearance in which reality presents itself to one's nature, grows in intensity of desire and singleness of mind through communication with one's *ishṭa-devatā*, or chosen deity, until it becomes transcendental worship – worship without object or distinction.

The transcendental state of consciousness is marked by a sense of the Void, cosmic spacelessness. Rituals lead ultimately to concentration on the point (Bindu), the centre at which all experience, all being, is compacted into its utmost concentration – to implode back into its origin.

'Ritual time' is conceived of as resembling the great *kalpas*, cosmic cycles of creation, preservation and dissolution, during which, at the *truṭi*, the atomic point of time, regarded as one ten thousand millionth of a second, space and time return to their origin – infinity. So in the preparations for ritual, calculations of conjunctions of planets and the rising of certain stars are used to determine *muhūrta*, the critical moment, *8–11*
which if missed will not recur for that particular ritual cycle. *Muhūrta* is the precise, astronomically determined instant, the sanctified time of auspicious beginnings.

Rituals concerned with the fundamentals of human existence – birth, marriage, death and the ancestors, the powers of good and evil – nourish the awareness of the hidden dimensions of life. Philosophy enquires into, but ritual acknowledges, the mysterious dimensions of existence. The works of art created for ritual use are not to be measured by aesthetic criteria, nor valued by acquisition. They are essentially functional.

They constitute a language, dense, precise and subtle, dealing with abstract forces. Their efficacy lies in the success with which their forms counter the negative forces of imbalance and barrenness with the positive powers of wholeness and vitality. The cave of the universe with its ceaseless births must be transcended by the mind, before the mind regains itself in the immensity beyond the womb.

Myth describes the ascent through ritual and meditation to realization of spiritual identity. Vishṇu in his incarnation as the fish is power asleep in the waters of creation. As the tortoise, he is the *axis mundi*, the stable and enduring centre that permits the churning of the ocean by gods and demons to produce the nectar of Being. As the boar, he roots out and delivers the Earth from deluge. As man-lion he is an ambivalent force, the avenger who emerges between light and dark, between civilization and the wild, to devour the oppressor. There follow his incarnations as man half-conscious of divinity and man the Enlightened. Vishṇu *is* all these incarnations, but he retains *Viśvarūpa*, his Cosmic Form in which he is the universe itself, the radiance beyond our seeing, blazing with the brightness of a thousand suns.

One inference that can be drawn from the myth of the incarnations of Vishṇu is that all life is related. The role of the animal in Indian myth and religion generally points to this, for divinity and animal-nature are never seen as opposed but as points on a continuum. Animals are worshipped, whether as vehicles of deities, like the bull of Śiva, or as their representatives, like the cat who is associated with the goddess of childbirth, Ṣaṣṭhi. Animal grace and power are used as metaphors for aspects of divinity. Śiva's massive causal strength is conveyed by his mount, the noble snow-white bull. The goddess Durgā confronts the dark forces in battle astride a lion or a tiger, a creature of grace and ferocity. Wise elephant-headed Gaṇeśa has as his vehicle the modest mouse which patiently overcomes great obstacles. Gaṇeśa is worshipped as the symbol of primordial power and spiritual equilibrium, and as such is a starting point for the process of human divinization.

Buddhism, in its approach to the interconnection of sentient beings, is more concerned with the self-evolving individual within the species. In the *Jākatas*, the folk legend derived apocrypha, Buddha has had previous earthly lives as bird, stag, jackal, horse, elephant, each of which creatures shares in self-determination.

All divine being is potentially immanent. All beings are witnesses to the great flux that they join at birth. All beings are alike in this, that each, according to its nature, is given the freedom and responsibility to act in harmony with the purpose for which it is destined. We are each at a point in our own transformation. There is a gentle acuity of observation and development of the ethical sense which can allow a new state of consciousness to open – a state which can change our vision of the universe; and in this state of openness, a transformation to a higher plane becomes possible.

In this process of expanding one's awareness one must unfold one's inner, feminine soul, as we learn from the lives of Caitanya, Ramakrishna and many others. Each one of us has the power to experience the totality of being and becoming.

The creative act measures out into structures that which is essentially immeasurable. By the processes of ritual art the undifferentiated is made perceptible. First, a propitious time is sought. The cosmic forces must be appropriately aligned and favourable. Then the maker will purify the body by bathing, libations, ascetism of diet or fasting, and continence. By withdrawal from sensual distraction, the maker is enabled to build up through meditation and concentration the particular image or aspect of the deity that he wishes to represent or materialize. After the visualization is accomplished the auspicious materials must be sought by divination and prepared with rites of purification.

The icon or diagram so created is considered as a presence, an appearance of deity. It is born of abstinence and meditation from flawless materials, each stage of its preparation ritually sanctified. Then, at a chosen instant, in accordance with the conjunction of stars, the deity is induced to 'breathe' (*prāṇa-praṭisthā*) into the image, and the image comes awake to worship. Its maker, the carrier of its conception, has played his part.

When a new worshipper enters the ritual, after cleansing his body with consecrated water, he explores self through the rites of *saṅkalpa*, 'resolution', *bodhana*, 'awakening', *āchmana*, 'sipping the sacred water', *samarpaṇa*, 'dedication', *āsana*, 'assuming the sitting posture', *bhūta-sūddhi*, 'purification of elements', *nyāsa*, 'rite of touching', *tarpaṇa*, 'libation of water', *añjali*, 'offering', *āratī*, 'waving of lighted oil-lamps and other ingredients', ending with *visarjana*, 'dissolution'. Intended as reverence, at its finest ritual awakens a direct apprehension of what is being reverenced.

From the practise of ritual arises a new phenomenon. This is the disappearance of the difference between the sacred and the profane. The two categories are ultimately merged in a unified and fully developed world-view. The great chain of sentient beings, the *jīvas*, are linked in the spiral of evolution towards finer and finer awareness. Creation is conceived of as the multiplication of categories emerging from a source into which all categories are intended to dissolve again.

To dissolve oneself systematically into the essence – this is the unifying purpose of all Indian ritual. The ritual impulse everywhere is essentially an impulse towards reverence of the life-force and self-identification with it.

The inert stone becomes a vital sign in the egg-shaped *Svayaṁbu-liṅga*
3, 4 or *Brahmāṇḍa*, or the rounded *Śālagrāma*. These objects need no special display to give them their broad universality of meaning. They are set down simply under the open sky beside the banyan tree. A mountain spring that runs red for five days is venerated as a natural shrine of Mother Earth.

Ritual develops a symbolic language of vertical and horizontal lines, dots and circles. In the art of ritual every form, every action, every surrounding circumstance or event, is correlated. Forms and names 'encircle', as it were, their source, interlinked at their creative point of origin. The source itself is unnameable, pre-logical and pre-formal – 'an archetype of the archetypes'. It is the belief in a cosmic order which can *5, 6* be mirrored in ritual that leads the *śilpi-yogin* to involve him- or herself as a part of the mystery. For without complete identification of one's being there can be no revelation of the great truth.

The *śilpi-yogin* like the surrealist reveals a hidden world. The symbols and patterns of ritual art, however, are maps of spiritual growth, while the dream world of the surrealist expresses a sense of flux, for it is contingent on the passing, shifting moment.

Myths gather around ritual objects and icons. Power appears to concentrate in their presence as much from the epiphanic experiences to which they give rise as from any inherent energy of the objects themselves. The relationship between self and focus of worship is therefore a continually recharging one, as the object draws power from the energy of the reverence it receives. It is popularly believed that the finer the qualities of reverence an object receives, the greater will be its capacity to generate reverence. This is so much the case that the reputation for power of a particular icon or shrine may be unrelated to its antiquity, physical appearance or authorship.

In general, however, it is considered that the older a particular ritual object is, the more potent it is likely to be. And if at some point it has been handled or used by an especially saintly individual, the more highly will it be estimated, since he or she will have transmitted to it a special power.

The classical icon is regarded in much the same way as the popular image, the main difference being the wider range of iconography and the higher degree of formal refinement of the classical representation. There is, for example, a characteristic stance and gesture to represent each aspect of the deity. The process of making the icon is in itself an intricately ritualized procedure. The principles behind classical and folk-tribal image-making are, nonetheless, basically the same.

In the Indian countryside ritual is still vigorous and prolific, and visual symbols are simple, vital and immediate. Everywhere the splash of scarlet *sindūra* on a wayside stone or shrine signals the approach to sacred space. Any village celebrates the rites of local nature deities.

It is in the performance of community worship that the classical tradition parts company with the vernacular, for in Hinduism each rite is performed by a member of the priestly class who is especially skilled. However long the process may take, each minute stage and each participant is carefully prepared, for, were a negative force, however slight, to enter, it would harm the integrity of the procedures and the worship would suffer as a result. The final mantras by which divinity is 'brought awake' literally transmute the work of art into the deity.

Indian ritual art may differ in detail according to locality, but not in expressiveness, or in range of symbolism, or in wealth of myth and dramatic enactment. It connects with subterranean rivers of the psyche in us all. Its roots lie in the neolithic, and among its tributary sources are pre-Brahminical cults. The Great Goddess retains her powers.

The power of the feminine is ambivalent. It guards and ripens, yet it also destroys. In icons of fertility the Mother is central, and the child, a biological second, if present, recedes, having undergone parturition from its source – only to collaborate more formally in the relationship. The resultant tension in immobility is the primeval root of beauty. Biological realities stand for metaphysical realities: relationships are universalized.

Biological symbolism works at more than one level. It is a communication arising from the cult, but developed within established religion it becomes a subtle, esoteric language. A basic and 'gut' symbolism may lead us at the unconscious level to the psychic 'point of return' at which the mysteries take place.

Much of the symbolism of nature worship is pre-iconic. The hallowed
16 pit or cave, the breast-stone or well, the bloodlike splash of vermilion,
39 the circle-glyph of fullness, the female triangle of fertility, signal to us

with startling vividness and immediacy, and are as natural to the Indian landscape as the land itself.

The brimming earthen grain-store and the filled womb – these *are* life, and also the carriers of divinity. As Mircea Eliade has written, 'The wealth arising from the earth is not just capital but the bearer of her sacredness.' Whether in indigenous or sanskritic ritual, divinity is
signalled by the rounded earthen jar, heavy-laden with water, the fluid *32–5*
of life. Indispensable to any rite are the *pūrṇa-ghaṭa* and *maṅgala-ghaṭa*,
consecrated water pots containing sacred Ganges water, the ritually *21, 127*
prepared waters of purification and blessing.

The symbolism of the filled jar is of vital sap, amniotic fluid, the
primal waters of creation. The feminine here encompasses all. As Erich *38*
Neumann has pointed out: 'If we survey the whole of the symbolic sphere determined by the vessel-character of the Archetypal Feminine, we find that in its elementary and transformative character the Feminine as 'creative principle' encompasses the whole world. This is the totality of nature in its original unity, from which all life arises and unfolds, assuming, in its highest transformation, the form of the spirit.' (*The Great Mother*, tr. Ralph Manheim)

The making of the pot or image is conceived of as in itself an offering, or as an act of self-consecration to the deity. In popular worship, the votive offering *becomes* the deity through the act of offering. Offered, it is left beside the pond or tree to dissolve back into the materials of which it was made. Such simplicity of worship survives alongside the immense expansion of ritualism in India.

The entire cosmic system is present, as it were, within the individual, waiting only to be actualized. Resonating on many levels, ritual enacts the relation between spirit and matter, between part and whole. Ritual neither restricts nor confines. It directs attention from the inessential to the essential, and shows the path to freedom and integration through its shapely rhythms of discipline.

As the festival icon of Durgā is worshipped and then ritually

101 relinquished when it is cast into the water at the time of *visarjana*, so consciousness builds towards its own dissolution, its relinquishment in the *samarasa*, the undifferentiated essence where there is neither 'mine' nor 'thine', but only Bliss-consciousness. As Ramakrishna has expressed it: 'The salt doll and its selfhood melt at the first encounter with the ocean.' The metaphysical dissolution of part into the Whole is the end of all ways.

'In atomic physics', writes Fritjof Capra (in *The Turning Point*), 'the observed phenomena can be understood only as correlations between various processes of observation and measurement, and the end of this chain of processes lies always in the consciousness of the human observer. The crucial feature of quantum theory is that the observer is not only necessary to observe the properties of an atomic phenomenon, but is necessary even to bring about these properties. My conscious decision about how to observe, say, an electron will determine the electron's properties to some extent. If I ask it a particle question, it will give me a particle answer; if I ask it a wave question, it will give me a wave answer. The electron does not *have* objective properties independent of my mind. In atomic physics the sharp Cartesian division between mind and matter, between the observer and the observed, can no longer be maintained. We can never speak about nature without at the same time speaking about ourselves.'

Starting in the immediate and perceptible, ritual brings forth the vision of the *ishṭa*, the desired object, and piece by piece, the picture is completed, until at last a moment comes when the vision is totally changed, and subject and object, Śiva and Śakti, become one. In the words of the famous Bengal boatman's song:

In search of Thee, I found myself.

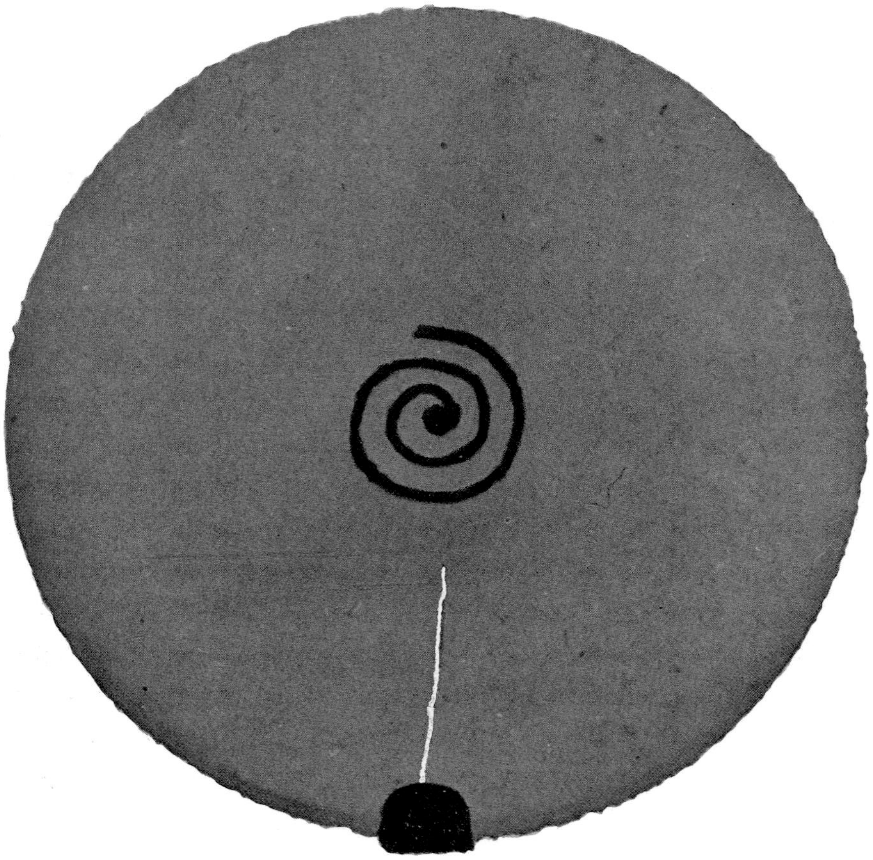

Chapter One

Primal Form

Throughout India, from time immemorial, an idiom of simple forms has provided the language of inward searching – a vocabulary of signs to express the human relationship with the universe. *Śilpi-yogins*, ritual artists, have recognized symbolic forms in natural objects such as river-rounded stones – *Śālagrāma* – representing the Universal Consciousness, or egg-shaped stones – *Brahmāṇḍa* – representing eternal Reality in absolute form. The builders of the Vedic fire altars and painters of yantras combine geometric shapes into configurations that create sacred space and concentrate vital energies. Cosmogonic diagrams chart a pathway of evolution which is retraced by the psyche during ritual worship – a return to the source. Planetary diagrams determine the correct timing for the performance of the ritual.

The Sanskrit texts stress the necessity of inner visualization to discover the true nature of reality. The vision of the *śilpi-yogins* represents a supreme form of concentration, most especially when ritual performance is combined with the methods of yoga. *Śilpi-yogins* are not, properly speaking, innovators or creators; they express an order that already exists (*sarvam*), of which they are a part, and so represent it to the world. In this 'giving back' to the world, the process through which the artist realizes him- or herself in relation to the whole is much more important than the work of art that is created. For the ritual artist, the making of a work of art is a way of living by which the principles of cosmic order are experienced and communicated.

In the background of the whole process of creation is the Primal Matter pulsating with its own life, vibrating with inherent force, seeded with potentialities. Creative heat, starting a new vibration in the Primal Matter, gives rise to creative desire, the will-to-be which acts as the seed of mind, the imaginative principle, and from this follows the entire series of creations of visible, tangible forms.

NASADIYA SŪKTA, ṚIG VEDA

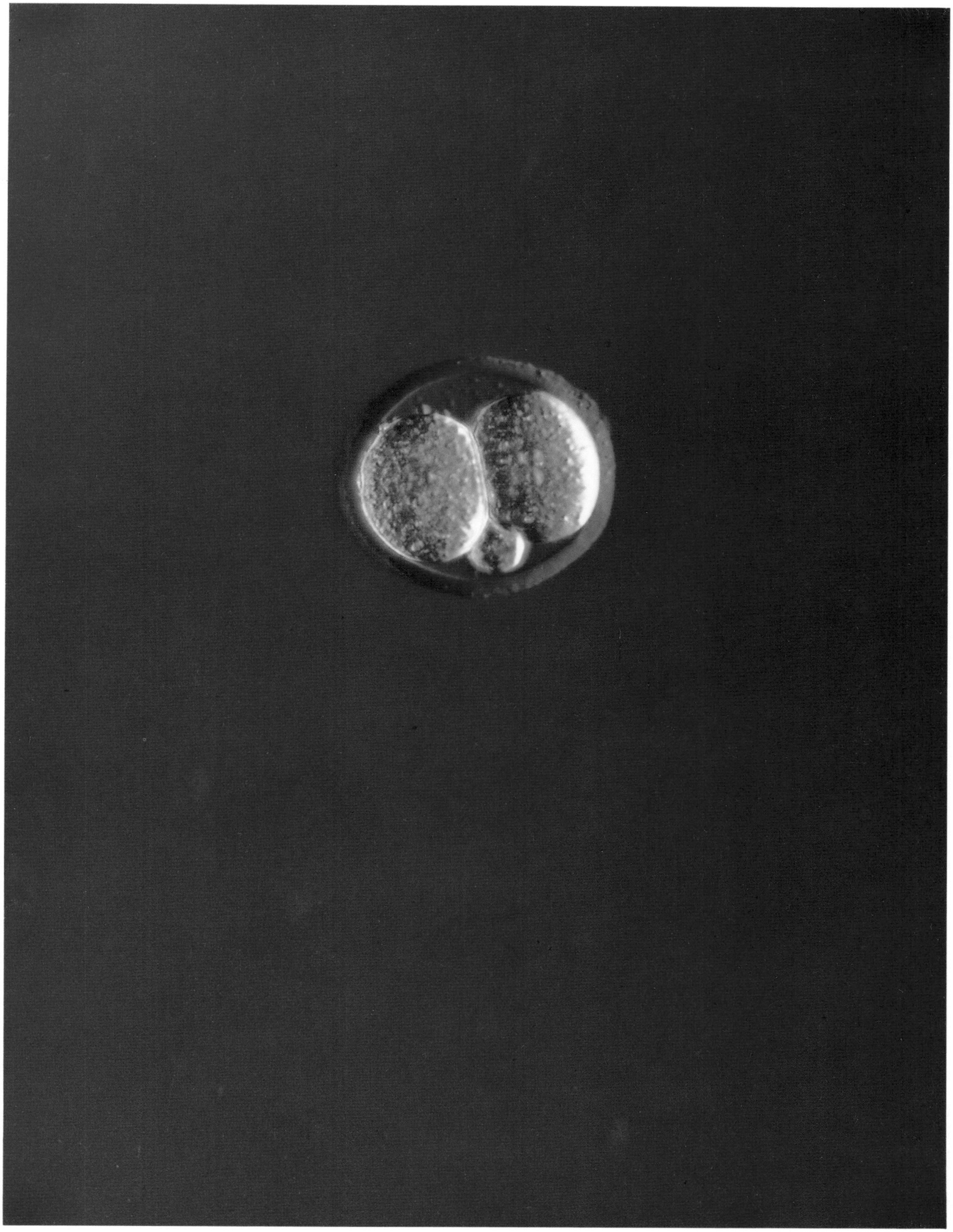

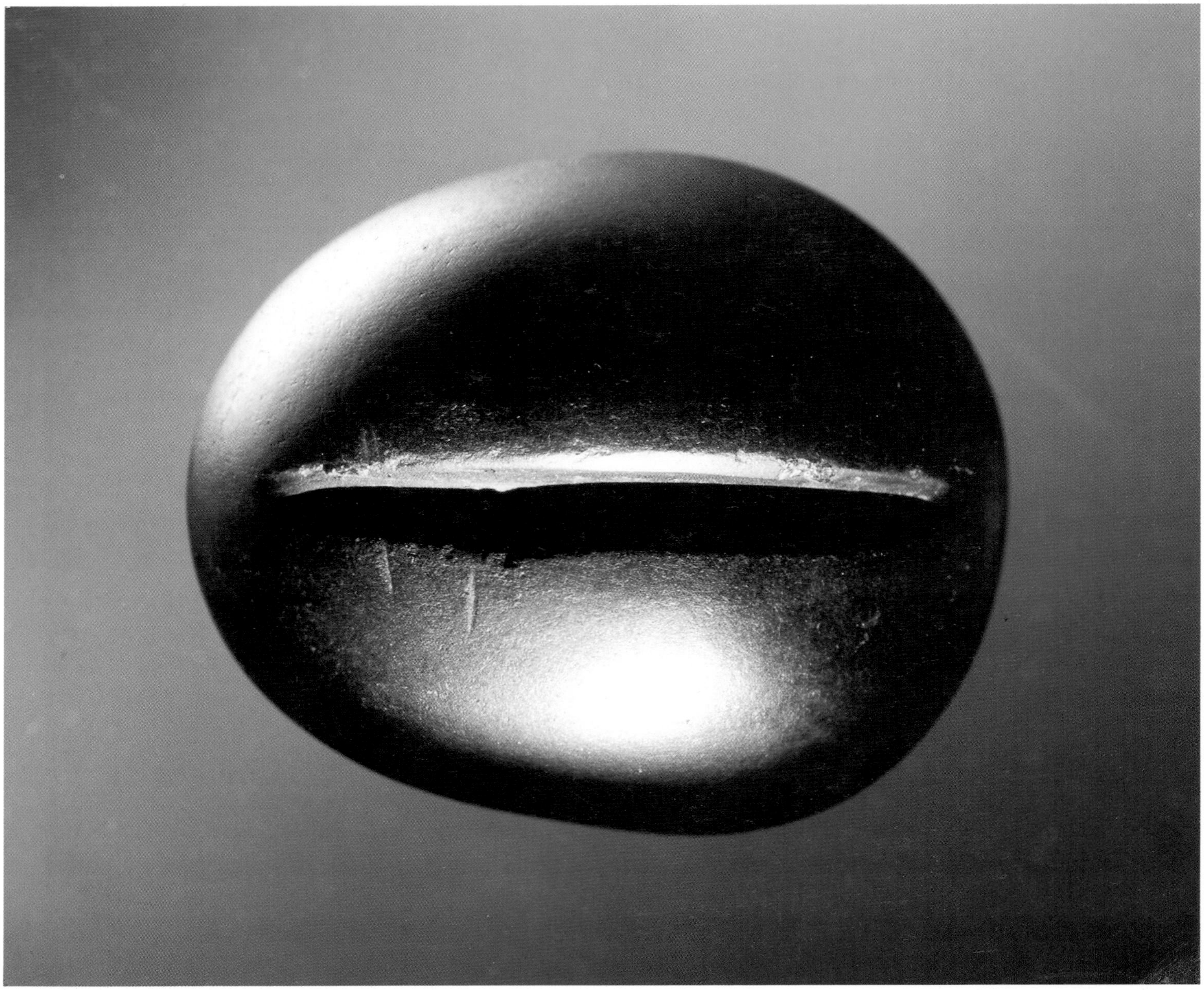

PREVIOUS PAGE
2 Dividing human cell. Photograph by Lennart Nilsson

3 Śālagrāma or Nārāyaṇa, symbol of Vishṇu, second god of the Hindu trinity, and of Universal Consciousness. (Banaras. Natural stone with carved incision)

4 Brahmāṇḍa, or Cosmic Egg, the 'first embryo' and symbol of all-pervasive reality. (Banaras. Natural stone with flash-patterns)

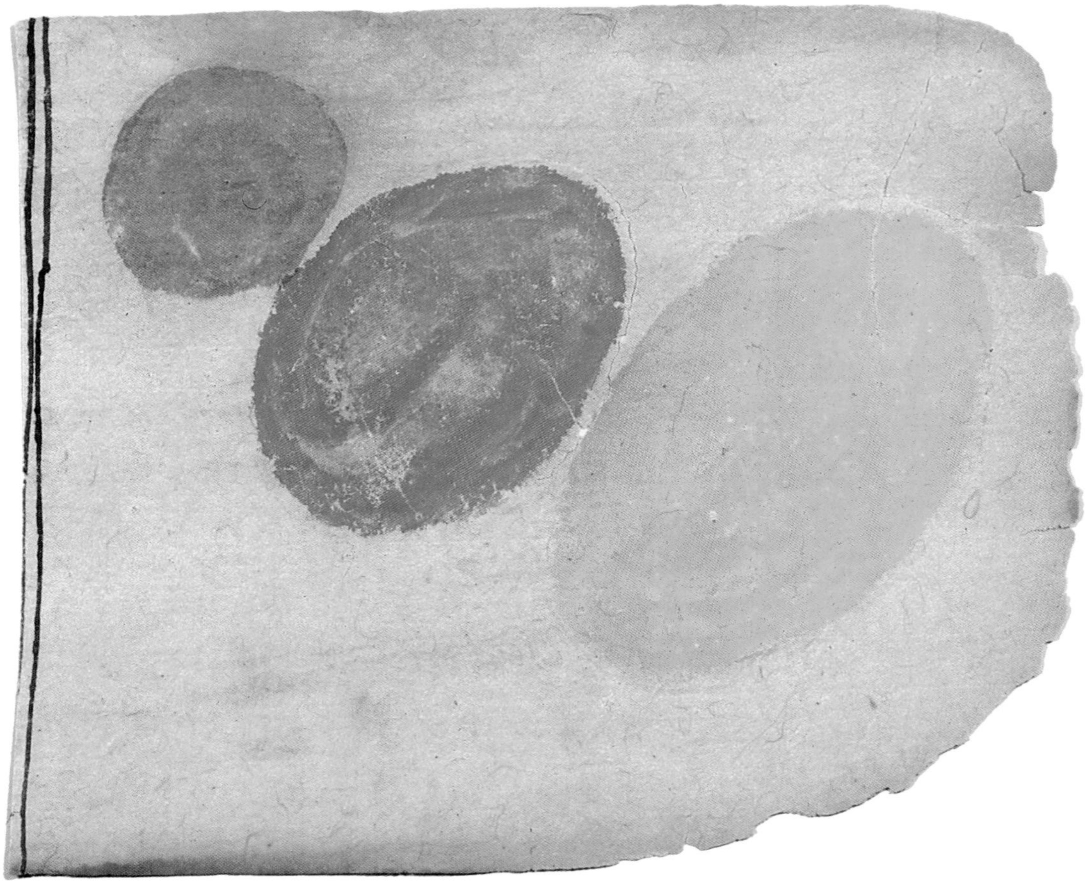

The unfolding of the universe with the multiplication of categories. The five grosser elements, at the point of emergence of the world of the five senses, play an essential role in ritual

5 Diagram of the evolving cosmic order, emanating by means of the disequilibrium of three forces, *sattva*, *rajas* and *tamas*, traditionally represented by the colours red, yellow and green. (Rajasthan, *c.* 1900. Gouache on paper)

6 Diagram representing the five *bhūtas* or grosser elements, earth, water, fire, air and ether, evolved by a process of condensation from the five *tanmātras* or subtle energies. (Rajasthan, 18th century. Ink and colour on paper)

(५) सोम प्रजापतिः "भूतानि"

आत्मा (चित्)		प्राणाः (हितम्)		पशवः (उपहितम्)	
पुरुषः (अक्षरः)	प्रकृतिः (क्षरः)	उक्थः (प्राणः)	अर्कः प्राणश्चित्रावु	अन्नम्	वितानम्
सोमः (अपरिणामी)	अन्नम् (परिणामी)	आनन्दम्	भूतानि अक्षितमः		

पृथ्वीपदस्मात्परं मत्याग्नि सोममयम् (अन्न मयम्)

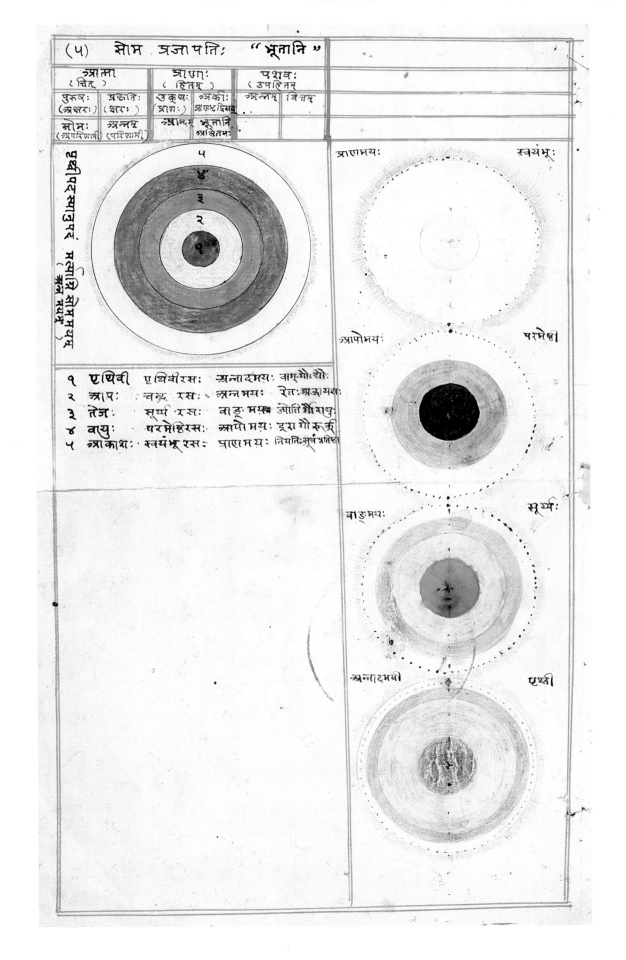

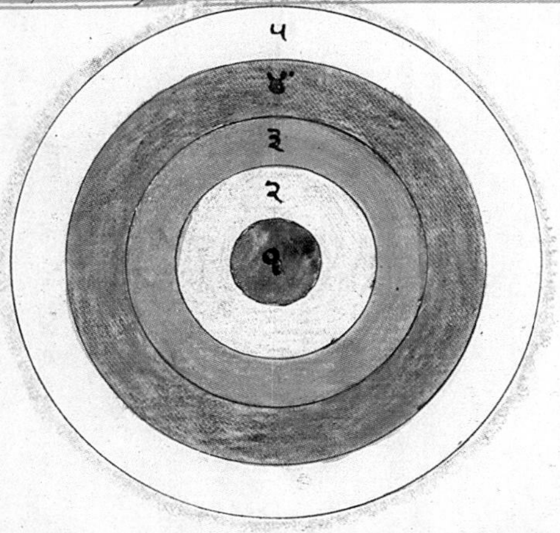

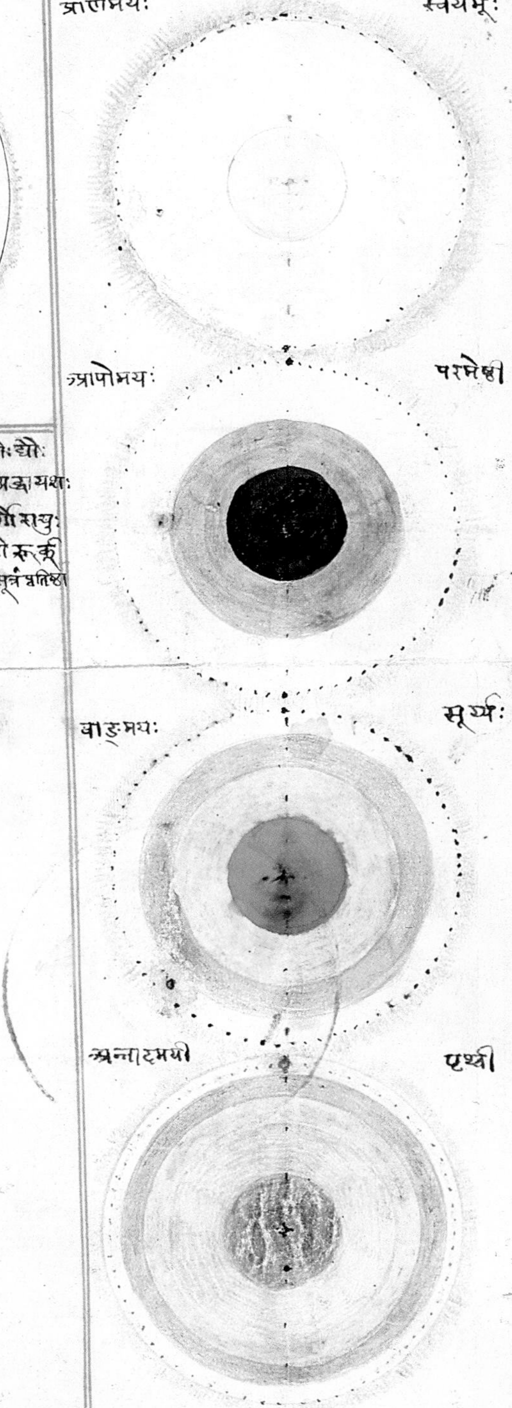

१	पृथिवी	पृथिवीरसः	अन्नादमयः	वाग्गौः द्यौः
२	आपः	चन्द्र रसः	अन्नमयः	रेतः श्रद्धा यशः
३	तेजः	सूर्य्य रसः	वाङ्मयः	ज्योतिर्गौरायुः
४	वायुः	परमेष्ठिरसः	आपोमयः	इरा गौ रूर्क्
५	आकाशः	स्वयंभू रसः	प्राणमयः	नियतिः सूत्रं प्रतिष्ठा

(१) ब्रह्म प्रजापतिः "वेदाः"

आत्मा (चित्)		प्राणाः (हितम्)		पशवः (उपहितम्)	
पुरुषः (अपरिणामी)	प्रकृतिः (परिणामी)	उक्थ (प्राणः)	अर्काः (प्राणभृद्विराट्)	अन्नम्	वित्तम्
ब्रह्मा	प्राणः	ब्रह्म	वेदाः (अक्षितयः)		

पृथ्वी-पदस्यानुपदं प्राण मयम्

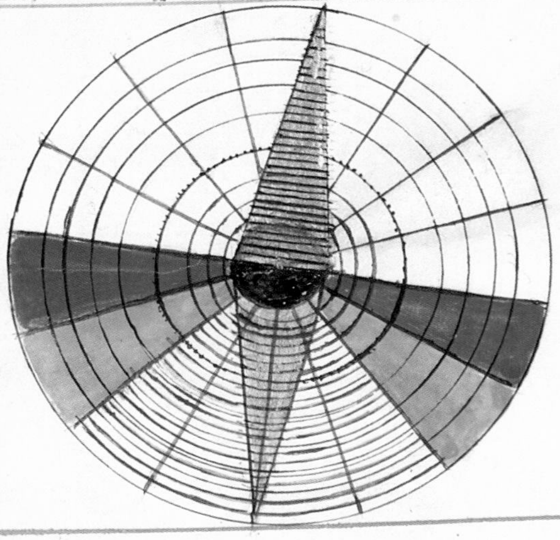

(२) विष्णु प्रजापतिः "लोकाः"

आत्मा (चित्)		प्राणाः (हितम्)		पशवः (उपहितम्)	
पुरुषः (अपरिणामी)	प्रकृतिः (परिणामी)	उक्थ (प्राणः)	अर्काः (प्राणभृद्विराट्)	अन्नम्	वित्तम्
विष्णुः	आपः	रजः	लोकाः (अक्षितयः)		

पृथ्वी-पदस्यानुपदम्-आपोमयम्

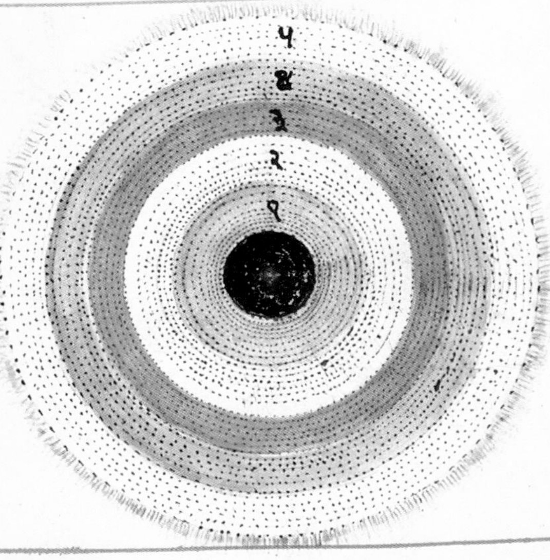

१- पृथ्वी अग्निः अग्निः अन्नात्

(३) इन्द्र प्रजापतिः "प्राणाः"

आत्मा (चित्)		प्राणाः (हितम्)		पशवः (उपहितम्)	
पुरुषः (अपरिणामी)	प्रकृतिः (परिणामी)	उक्थ (प्राणः)	अर्काः (प्राणभृद्विराट्)	अन्नम्	वित्तम्
इन्द्रः	वाक्	वषट्कारः	प्राणाः गावः अहानि अक्षितयः		

पृथ्वी-पदस्यानुपदं वाङ् मयम्

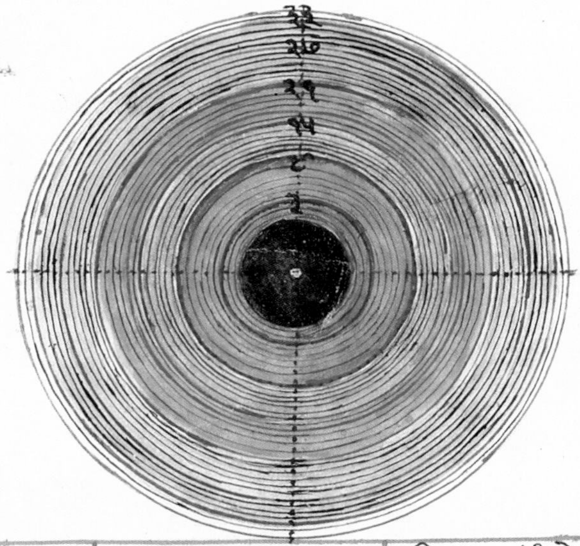

सहस्रं गावः १०००	३० गावः – १ अहः	१ त्रिवृत् ९ स्तोमः
त्रयस्त्रिंशदहानि ...३३	६ अहानि – १ स्तोम	२ पञ्चदशः १५ "
षट् स्तोमाः ...६	६ स्तोमाः – १ वषट्कार	३ सप्तदशः १७ "
एको वषट्कारः ...१		४ एकविंशः २१ "
		५ त्रिणवः २७ "

(४) अग्नि प्रजापतिः "देवाः"

आत्मा (चित्)		प्राणाः (हितम्)		पशवः (उपहितम्)	
पुरुषः (अपरिणामी)	प्रकृतिः (परिणामी)	उक्थ (प्राणः)	अर्काः (प्राणभृद्विराट्)	अन्नम्	वित्तम्
अग्निः	अन्नादः	यज्ञः ४।४।१२।५।१२	देवाः ३३ अक्षितयः		

पृथ्वी-पदस्यानुपदम् अमृताग्निसोममयम् (अन्नाद मयम्)

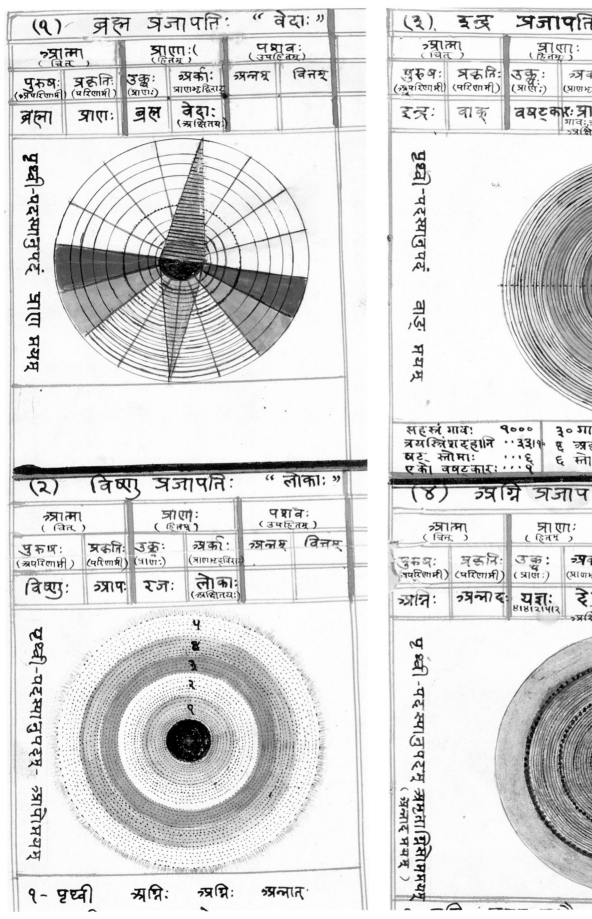

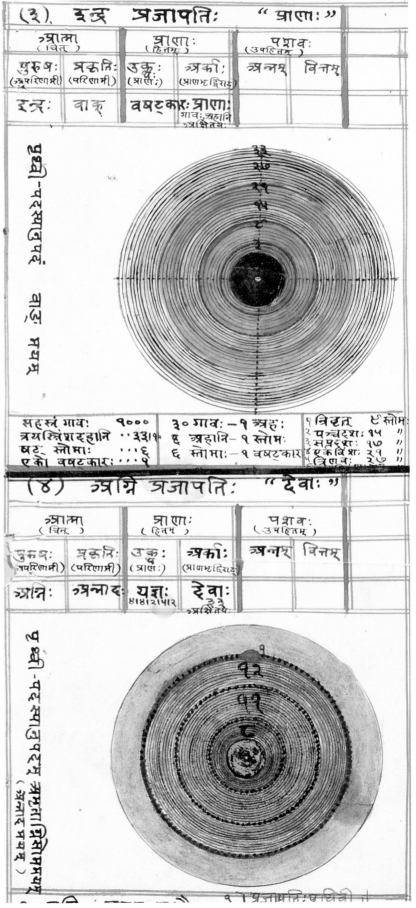

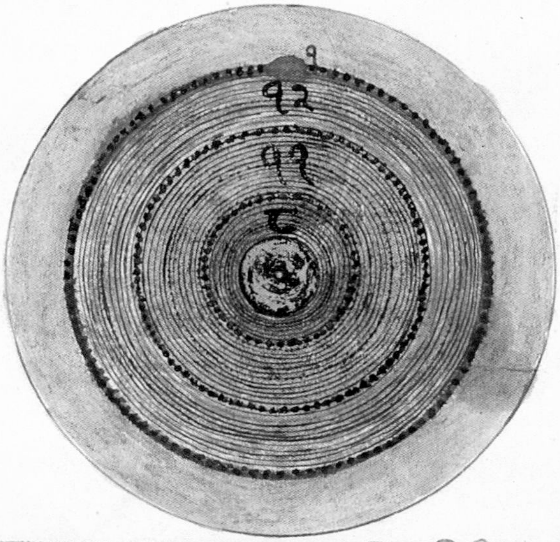

१ प्रजापतिः पृथिवी ।

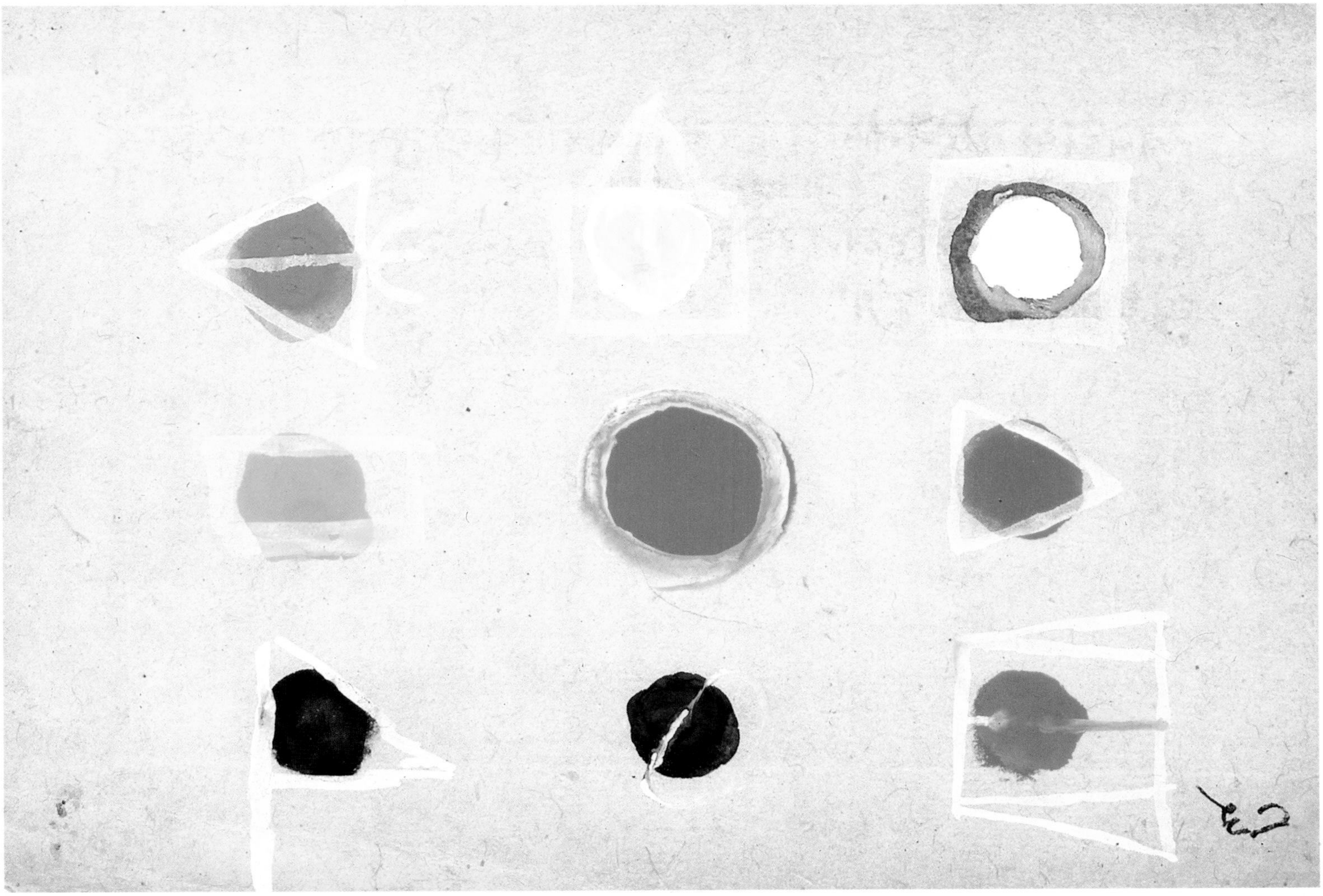

7 Diagram of the evolution of the cosmos according to the Vedic tradition, by which Prajāpati, 'lord of creatures', creates the world by 'heating' himself. (Rajasthan, 18th century. Ink and colour on paper)

8 Nava-graha, the presiding nine planets of paramount importance for the calculation of appropriate times for rituals and sacrifices. (Rajasthan, *c.* 1900. Gouache on paper)

Heat – the inner and the outer fire – is transformative energy. The auspicious moment for the performance of ritual is determined by a calculation of correspondences

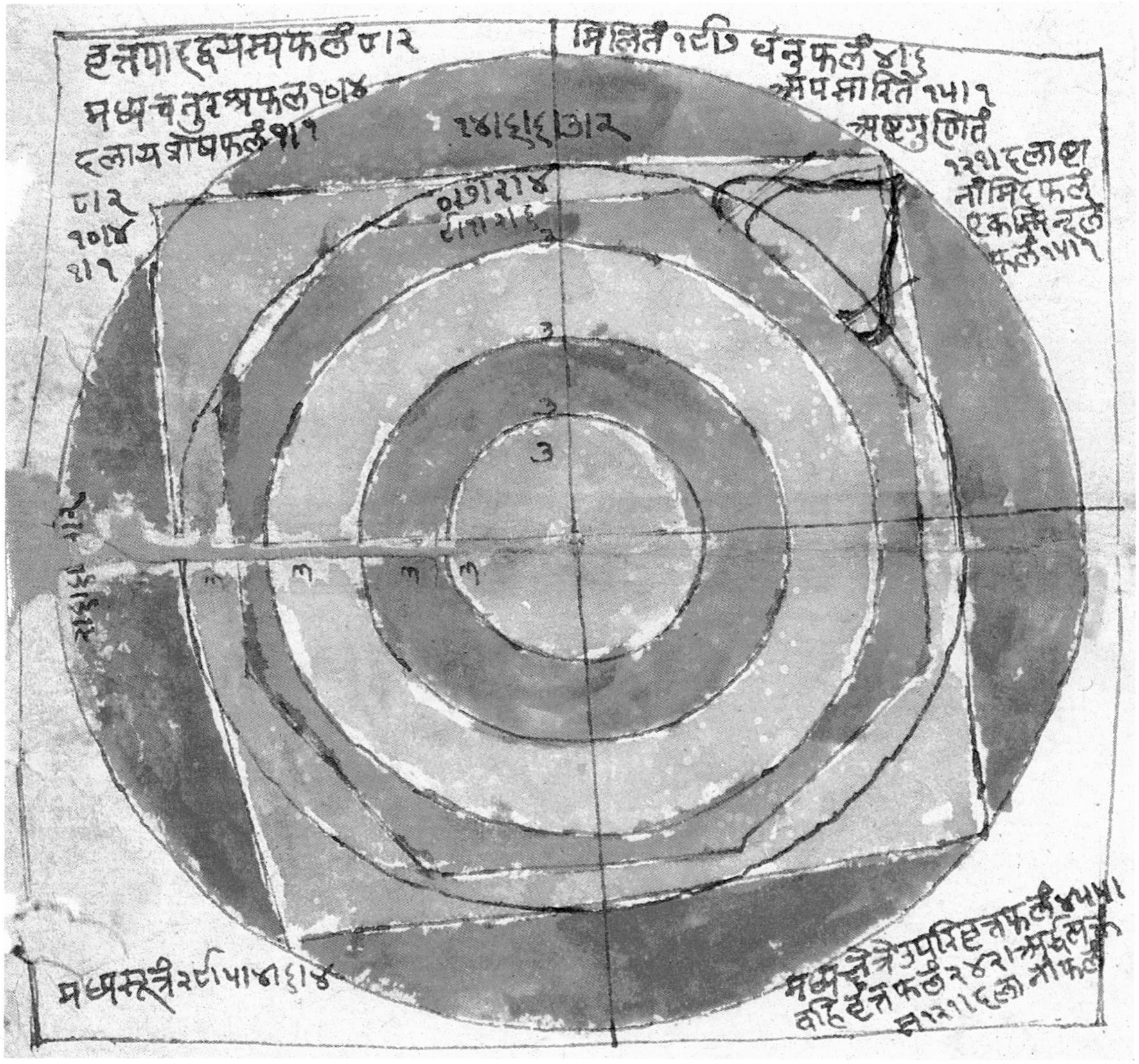

9 Chart of the twelve zodiacal divisions in relation to ritual. (Rajasthan, *c.* 18th century. Ink and colour on paper)

10, 11 Astrograms illustrating the twelve zodiacal divisions, for use in computations of the correct timing of rituals. (Rajasthan, *c.* 18th century. Ink and colour on paper)

बुचंद्रेबुक्रविघातंनिरीसयेत॥इतिवायुस्फपतचंद्रचक्रं॥ चक्राकारे त्रिखंडे त्रिलवपरिमिता ता

तारका भ त्रिमध्ये॥तद्वा
धोरेत्तत्येशिशिरकि
रणाज्जन्मभंचिन्ननीयं॥
सौम्यैग्रामे स्ववाह्यांन
वनशनयोर्मध्यवाह्यो
क्रमेणाधार्यवेयुनचो
यें।भिजिरिपुन्नपतेमोर
वंधारख्यचक्रम॥इतिमो
टचक्रम॥अथवेटाचक्रम
चंद्रमानलवधिस्प्पानित्रिरा
वेनानिस्करोरि॥क्रमेक्रमेणगएंपते यावज्जोन्म र्क्षं स्थिते॥

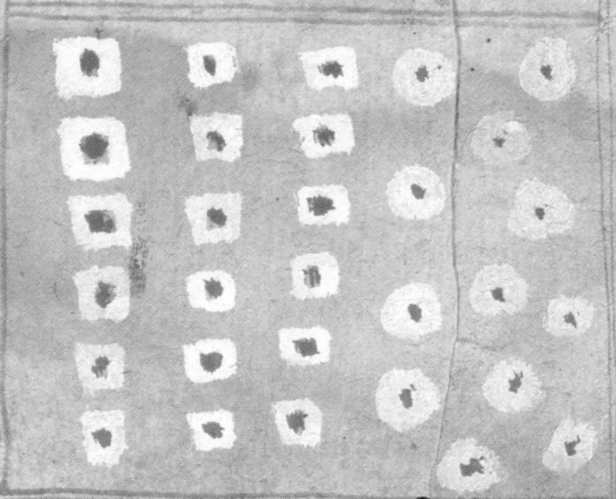

चक्राकारंलिखेच्चक्रंचतुर्नाडीकमध्यगं॥ततस्तेसा।तफलचा।च्चंवेटाचक्रेतुनिश्चितम॥मध्ये
त्रीणिगृहे शत्रुर्धार्यते ग्रहाद्वहि॥तत्परेणैव ग्राममध्ये तु चतुर्थे ग्रामवाह्यगे॥वैर्यकोमे
नष्टेषु शत्रुणांसाधनेषु च॥ चक्रे वेष्टेति विख्यात स्वरशास्त्रेषु कीर्तितम॥इतिवेटाचक्रं॥प्र
थग्रामचक्रम॥रेखोर्ध्वोतिर्यगाभ्यांस्यातत्रोतिर्यग्गृहे॥सर्वाग्राम्योतरेरेखे वर्णाम॥स तयार

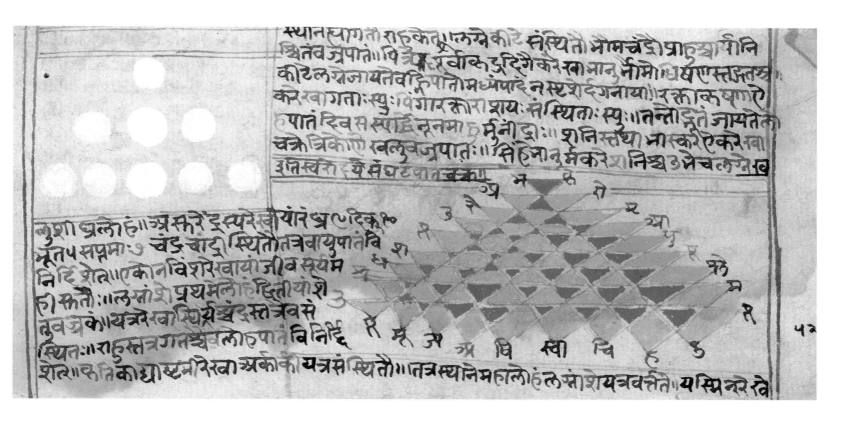

स्थानह्यागतौ राहुकेतू॥लग्नेकीटेसंस्थितौ भौमचंद्रौ प्राहुस्त्वासौनि
श्चितंवज्रपातं॥पित्रेयूर्वाल्दुद्दिगेकेरखा भानुर्नीमो॥धर्षणस्त्तजतत्र
कीटलग्नेजायतेवाह्निपातोमध्यंपादंनस्पृशेदंगनायाः॥रक्षाल्कषाणे
करखागताःस्युःपिंगारकौराशयःसंस्थिताःस्युः॥तन्त्तौदूतेजायतेतौ
हपातंदिवससपार्दिनूनमाहुर्मुनीद्राः॥ शनिस्तथा भास्करेऐकरेखा
चक्रेत्रिकोणेखलुवज्रपातः॥सिंहेभानुर्मकरेशानिश्चउभेचलग्ने ख
इतिस्वरोदयेसंघटपातचक्रम॥

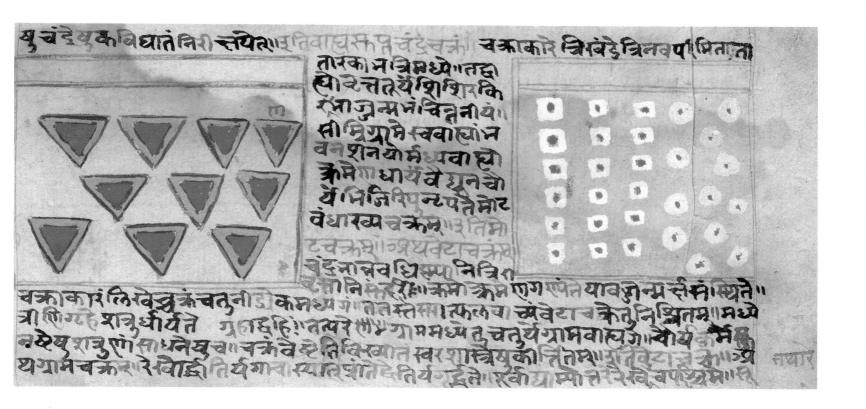

लुशीधृलोहं॥अस्करेद्रस्यरेखोयांरेधृ९दिकृ१०
मूतपसप्तमाः७ चंद्रवाद्रौस्थितौतत्रवायुपातंवि
निर्दिशेत॥एकोनविंशरेखायांजीवसूर्यम
हीसुतौः॥लग्नांशेप्रथमेलोहंद्वितीयांशे
तुवज्रकं॥यत्ररेखास्थितौ चंद्रस्तत्रैवसे
स्थितः॥राहुस्तत्रगतश्चैवलोहपातंविनिर्दि
शेत॥कृतिकाद्याष्टमीरेखाअर्काकीयत्रसंस्थितौ॥तत्रस्थानेमहालोहंलग्नांशेयत्रवर्त्तते॥यस्मिन्नरेखे ५२

In the world's oldest surviving ritual, the building of an immense fire altar is called 'the piling-up of Agni' – Agni being both altar and god. Agni the god of fire is also identified with the creator-god Prajāpati. The five layers of the altar correspond to the five 'sheaths' of the soul

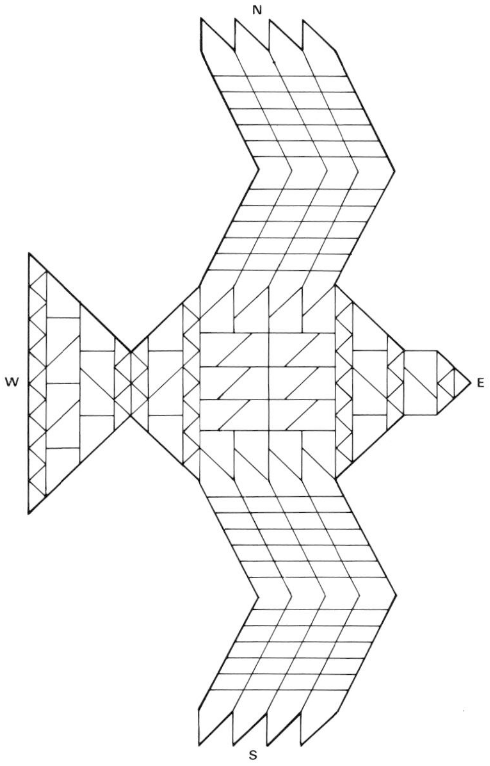

12 Bird-shaped altar for a fire sacrifice whose origin dates back some three thousand years. (Panjal, Kerala. Clay bricks)

13 Placing and consecrating pebbles on the fifth layer of the altar. (Panjal, Kerala)

14 Milk oblation performed at the north-western tip of the north wing of the bird-shaped fire altar. (Panjal, Kerala)

15 Diagram for the *yajña*, or fire sacrifice. (Rajasthan, *c.* 18th century. Ink and colour on paper)

Plate 2
A dividing reproductive cell is the potential source of approximately 6,000 billion cells of a human body, all collaborating in the common purpose of survival and reproduction – until they are dissolved again into their elements at the end of the human life. Underlying the perceptible reality of separate but interacting entities of the manifested world is another intuited reality, the reality of an all-inclusive dynamic continuum.

Plate 3
The Universal Consciousness (Nārāyaṇa) is represented here by the rounded stone known as a Śālagrāma. Nārāyaṇa is recognized within all human beings, all animals, all plants, all rivers, all mountains and all forests, all suns, stars and planets. No ritual worship can begin without the offering of water to Nārāyaṇa. Every human being is essentially Nara-Nārāyaṇa, 'nara' meaning 'individual consciousness', and 'ayana' meaning 'refuge' – the refuge of perfection. The primordial female kinetic energy (Śakti) and the correlative male principle of consciousness (Purusha) are united in this seed- or cell-like image.

Plate 4
The First Cause formed the Hiraṇya-garbha or 'Golden Womb', the Cosmic Egg which floated upon the surface of the primeval waters. In this egg-shaped Brahmāṇḍa we find represented Wholeness. The Brahmāṇḍa symbolizes the totality in which the male and female principles are eternally united.

Plate 5
The cosmic evolutionary cycle commences with the disturbance of the equilibrium of three forces which constitute the Primal Ground. They are *sattva*, the cohesive or unifying force, *rajas*, the creative energy, and *tamas*, the opposing force of mass or inertia. In the cosmic cycle no unity is absolute, but each is a synthesis of opposite principles, whose potential disequilibrium is neutralized by the principle of unity. The colours representing the three forces are specified in the *Svetasvatara Upanishad* (iv, v) as red for rajas, black for tamas and white for the cohesive force, sattva. The three-fold forces are reflected in ritual as the three phases of Universal Becoming.

Plate 6
In the Sāṁkhya (*c.* 500 BC) account of the evolution of the cosmos, Nature (Prakṛiti) evolves from subtle to gross forms. The geometry of the diagram of the five discs represents this evolutionary process at the point where the subtle energies – which are of liberation, or sound potential; of impact, or touch potential; of radiant heat and light, or colour potential; of viscous attraction, or taste potential; of cohesive attraction, or smell potential – condense to become the five grosser atoms, which are ether (*vymon*), air (*marut*), fire (*tejas*), water (*ap*) and earth (*kshiti*). The five elements play an essential role in ritual. The vessel is placed on an earth-pedestal; it is filled with holy water; it is worshipped with flame, sound, and perfumes.

Plate 7
Cosmogonic plans combine early, Vedic (*c.* 1500 BC) and later (*c.* 500 BC) Sāṁkhya metaphysical concepts, embodying these ideas in abstract configurations based on mathematical relationships. The Sāṁkhya contribution here is the evolution of subtle energies (*tanmātras*) into gross physical elements (*bhūtas*). The Vedic account of evolution (represented by the spoked circle at top left) concerns the 'lord of creatures' Prajāpati.

The Changeless Person, Purusha, the male principle, and transcendental Nature, Parā-Prakṛiti, the female principle, manifest as the lord of progeny, Prajāpati, who is the substratum of the universe. Prajāpati creates the world by heating himself (*tapas*, heat, is the spiritual power gained through ascetism), and in this is identified with Agni (primordial, sacrificial and ritual fire), as also with the gods

Vishṇu, Brahmā and Candra who likewise incorporate the universe.

'Heat' is also the source from which emanate the natural laws personified as Indra, the celestial lord.

The observable activity of each individual is viewed as combustion and is also identified with Agni, while the activities of the spiritual self are identified with Soma, the fermented-juice offering.

Plates 8–11

One of the 'meanings' carried by abstract ritual diagrams is the interrelationships of ritual 'space' and ritual 'time'. Although the time-dimension is more explicit at some points than at others in the ritual, it is operative throughout the whole scheme of daily and yearly observances. The symbols of the astrograms relate to the lunar and solar calendar, and in particular to the lunar mansions (*nakṣatras*). Ritual 'units' correspond to time units astronomically calculated, and each is a microcosm of the rhythms of the universe. In practice, time units are also biological units marking the processes of human growth and agriculture. The diagrams mark seasonal celebration times, moments which affirm the fertile and joyous in life.

Plates 12–14

A few families of Nambudiri Brāhmins in Kerala continue to perform ancient Vedic rituals in which mantras play a large part. The chief of these ceremonies is the Agnicayana (building of the altar of fire, Agni). The present form of the ritual originated around 1000 BC, and is described in detail in Vedic texts. The performance lasts for twelve days, involving numerous recitations and chants, offerings of fermented juice, and oblations of milk and other substances. The rites require the construction of several fire altars, including a main altar built from more than a thousand bricks in the shape of a bird, the *śyena* or eagle.

The five layers of the bird-shaped fire altar became identified with the creator-god Prajāpati. Prajāpati created the world through his own dismemberment, the pieces of his body forming the various parts of the universe. In the construction of the fire altar, Agni-Prajāpati is reborn, and so is the sacrificer. The centre of the fire altar is named Ātman (self). Professor Frits Staal has suggested that it was the terminology of the Vedic fire altar which gave rise to the notion of the identity of Ātman and Brahman, the individual soul and the Universal Soul, one of the corner-stones of Indian philosophy.

A ritual of the fire altar consists in the placing and consecrating of river-rounded pebbles with special natural markings in the interstices of the bricks on the fifth layer of the altar. It is carried out by *yajmāna* and *adhvaya* priests – so named in the Vedic tradition.

Plate 15

Sacrificial rites (yajña = sacrifice) were an integral part of the Vedic way of life, and the source of the world's earliest hymns, earliest poetry, and probably the earliest drama and dance. The sacrifice is simple in performance but complex in meaning. The chart for the ritual (*c.* 18th century) indicates the traditional disposition of the seats for the yajmāna priest, his postures, gestures, responses, ablutions, the locations of the altars and other details of the ritual.

Chapter Two

Nature Worship

Nature worship is widespread in India. Natural features of the countryside such as mountains and hills, rivers and lakes, plants and trees are regarded as the abodes of deities and auspicious places for meditation. There are thousands of such spots whose special sanctity is enhanced by rituals performed there daily. Retreats in the Himalayas or on river banks shelter sages and yogis who are credited with universal knowledge, or revered as recipients of divine revelation. Especially hallowed are the sources and confluences of rivers.

Evidence of tree worship is found at Mohenjo-daro (*c.* 2500 BC), and it is still popularly believed that every tree has a 'tree-deity', a spirit who is worshipped with prayers, offerings and circumambulations. Trees are often garlanded and festooned with lights. Prayers are offered before cutting down a tree in order that the tree-spirit will not take vengeance on the cutter, for it is believed that trees have not only life but latent consciousness.

The great banyan is the most sacred of all trees. This fig tree is associated with spiritual understanding, and is the natural shelter for seekers after truth. It was under its branches that the Buddha received Enlightenment, hence it is known as the Bodhi tree. It was under the Śāla tree that Mahavira, the founder of Jainism, renounced the world, and the nineteenth-century mystic saint Ramakrishna experienced *samādhi* – the bliss state – beneath Pañchavati, 'Five Trees'.

The sun and the moon phases are personified as gods and goddesses; the deities have their animal incarnations. The difference between humankind and the animals, between animate and inanimate nature, is regarded as one of degree, not kind. While harmony with the natural world receives strongest emphasis in the worship practised in the countryside, it is a pervasive element in all Indian religious belief and ritual observance.

If ever I have somehow come to realize God, if the vision of God has ever been granted to me, I must have received the vision through this world, through man, through trees and birds and beasts, the dust and the soil.

RABINDRANATH TAGORE

16 Fig tree with marks of ritual worship. (Bakreswar Temple area, West Bengal)

17 Shrine with the deity installed at the foot of the tree. (Jaipur)

'Here under the banyan tree, the greatest problem of my life has been solved.'

Vivekananda

18 Female tree deity or Śālabhanjikā for temple worship. (Purana Mahadeva Temple, *c.* AD 973. Stone)

19 The Cosmic Tree set in a yantra diagram. (Illuminated manuscript page, Rajasthan, *c.* 18th century. Gouache on paper)

20 Tree-worship. (Illuminated manuscript page, Rajasthan, *c.* 18th century. Gouache on paper)

The sacred fig-tree of mythology is of two chief varieties, the banyan and the pipal. The Vedas *contain mention of a cosmic pipal tree with its roots in heaven and its branches and fruits reaching down to earth*

River banks are hallowed ground, and river steps are cross-points linking the rites with heaven and earth. During ritual bathing worshippers make oblation to the sun with finger-gestures and mantras

21 Worship on the river-bank with the ceremonial water pot. (Kangra painting, *c.* 18th century. Gouache on paper)

22, 23 Bathing and prayers at the Ganges. Whatever the source of the water used in ceremonial, it is always to be thought of as Ganges holy water. (Patna, Bihar)

Invocation of the sun

24 Agni, god of fire and ritual, and also the sacrificial fire. (Illuminated manuscript page, Rajasthan, *c.* 18th century. Gouache on paper)

25 Sūrya, the sun god, received by a virgin girl, Ushā, the Vedic Dawn. (Rajasthan, *c.* 18th century. Gouache on paper)

In a rite of great antiquity, two sacred birds are linked with the epic events of the Rāmāyaṇa. *In legend, they fly onward to the demon-kingdom of Lanka (modern Sri Lanka) invaded by Rama*

26 The temple rite of feeding the birds at Thirukkalikundram. (Tamil Nadu)

Plates 16, 17
Tree-shrines are a frequent sight in India. A pilgrim on his journey or a passer-by going about his daily life will see marks painted on a tree-trunk, or the image of a deity installed at the foot of the tree. No elaborate ritual is necessary; simply bowing down or throwing a flower will help to create inner adjustment and oneness with the environment.

Plate 18
The life that springs from earth and water, the first two elements of nature, is most powerfully and majestically represented by the tree. The spirit of the tree is personified by two classes of female figure, the *Śālabhanjikā* and the *Yakshī*. A Śālabhanjikā or Yakshī *is* the nature of the tree, not merely its symbol – hence offerings of food and flowers are made to the images. A frequently recurring motif in painting or sculpture is that of a maiden beneath the foliage of a tree, classically a beautiful young woman raising one hand to grasp a branch while standing on one foot, bending the supporting leg so that the other foot touches the trunk, or even twining one leg around it. In this image, the maiden represents the quickening power of nature. Some of the sculptures derive from a game, possibly an ancient springtime ritual, played by young girls, which virtually amounted to flirting with certain trees such as the Ashoka and the Śāla. In reaching up to break off twigs from the tree, the girl's foot would strike the trunk, and this, it is believed, would waken a deciduous tree from its dormant state. The ritual became so popular and applicable in such a wide range of religious connotations that the image was given the generic name of Śālabhanjikā; meaning 'she who breaks (a branch of) the Śāla tree'. The icon of Śālabhanjikā was made for propitiation in a temple.

Plate 19
The Cosmic Tree, the axis of creation. In Maharashtra in western India a virgin girl receives ritual worship standing on a yantra beneath a tree.

Plate 20
Two women are shown placing their hands against a tree in worship. Some trees are said to have a violent desire for the touch or attention of young women. Thus the Bakula (*Mimusope elengi*) bursts into flower when sprinkled with wine from the mouth of a young girl, while the Ashoka (*Saraca indica*) produces orange or scarlet blossom when touched by the foot of a maiden.

Plate 21
The sacred rivers of India are worshipped as the veins of Mother Earth, and rites are performed daily on their banks with water drawn in ceremonial water pots.

Plate 22
The ghāṭ, a great flight of steps leading to the water's edge, is regarded as a 'cross-point' connecting the rites with heaven and earth. India has innumerable sacred rivers, lakes and temple-tanks upon whose sides ghāṭs have been built. Ritual is performed there daily, as well as at auspicious times, on pilgrimages, and for important occasions such as initiations.

Plate 23
Visiting holy places or sacred rivers is one of the main religious duties of the Indian people. For Hindus, the bath is an act of purification, and its most effective form is the *arghya*, the morning bathe in the river, during which the worshipper makes oblation to the rising sun.

Plate 24
The power of the sun god, Sūrya, is called down to the sacrificial fire altar by the god of rituals, Agni, who is also the Fire itself. The fire ritual is being performed by both the deva (god) and asura (demon), two opposing powers struggling for ascendency.

Plate 25
Sūrya is represented riding the heavens on seven red horses, greeted by Ushā, Dawn. The Saurya sect worships the sun god as supreme deity, and temples dedicated to Sūrya are scattered all over India. The Konarak Temple in Orissa is the most magnificent, though partly ruined. The sūrya-namaskāra, salutation to the sun at sunrise, is made with finger gestures (mudrās) and mantras, while bathing.

Plate 26
The name of the rock-cut temple of Pakshitirtham at Thirukkalikundram means 'centre of the sacred birds'. For centuries two kites have been fed by priests at the appointed time in the morning. The legend is that these birds made their way each day from Banaras, nine hundred miles away, and fly on to Sri Lanka, in commemoration of the epic events of the *Rāmāyaṇa*.

Trumpet of natural shell, sounded at the commencement of the ritual

Chapter Three

Fertility Rites

In fertility rites the role of the Mother Goddess is supreme. Some of the earliest ritual objects are female figurines with pronounced breasts, hips and pubic triangles, like those discovered at Harappa and Mohenjo-daro in the Indus Valley which date from *c.* 2500 BC. In classical tradition the goddess Annapūrṇā is the giver of bountiful harvests and the provider of food, the Mother of Plenty.

Many benevolent goddesses protect and bless, and are propitiated especially during village festivals, or by young couples and their families to ensure happy marriage and children. Women have charge of the rites, and it is generally they who prepare the ritual drawings or model the clay figurines. Vessels for ritual worship are associated both by their shapes and their functions with the Mother Goddess, and with fertility.

Like the Mother Goddess, Lakshmī is known throughout India as the goddess of good fortune, beauty and success. Her other name is Padmā, the feminine form of the Sanskrit word *padma*, lotus. In early Buddhist sculpture the goddess is frequently represented standing on a lotus or surrounded by lotuses, bathed with water from pitchers. Just as the tree reaches toward the sky, the lotus grows upwards from the dark bed of a river, lake or pool to flower in the light and air on the water's surface. In this sense, the lotus is a transition symbol, but unlike Manasā, the Serpent Power, it is not dangerous and is inherently beautiful.

In the seasonal worship of the goddess Lakshmī, images are rarely used. She has no temples, but is worshipped in every household on all important occasions. It is customary to heap up rice in a bowl, decorate it with cowrie shells, and place it on a small wooden casket containing a coin, invoking the giver of good fortune and prosperity.

I shall support the whole world with the life-sustaining vegetables which shall grow out of my own body during a period of heavy rain.

MĀRKAṆḌEYA PURĀṆA

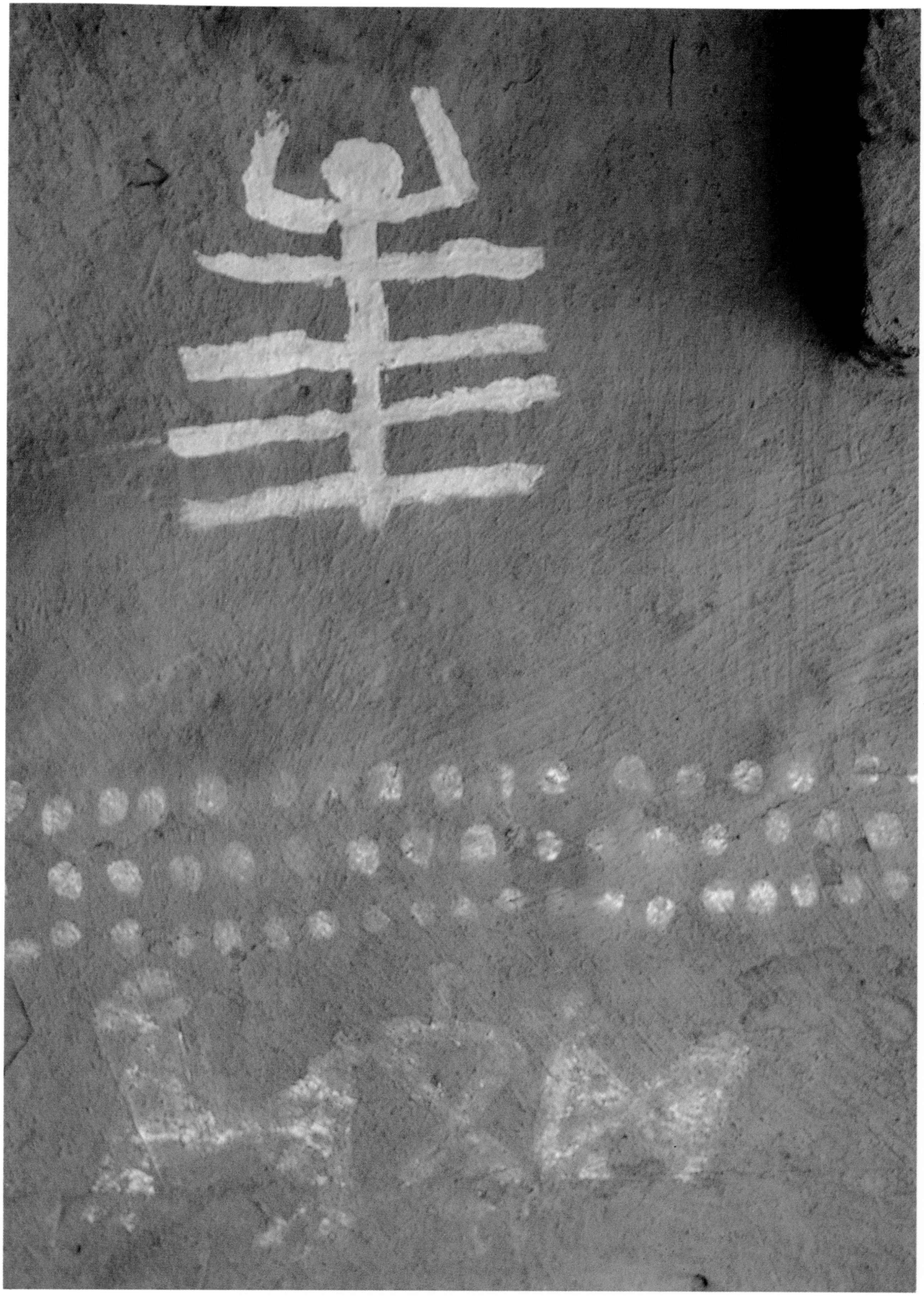

PREVIOUS PAGE

27 Invocation of the goddess of fertility and abundance, drawn on a mud wall. (Rajasthan. Rice-paste drawing)

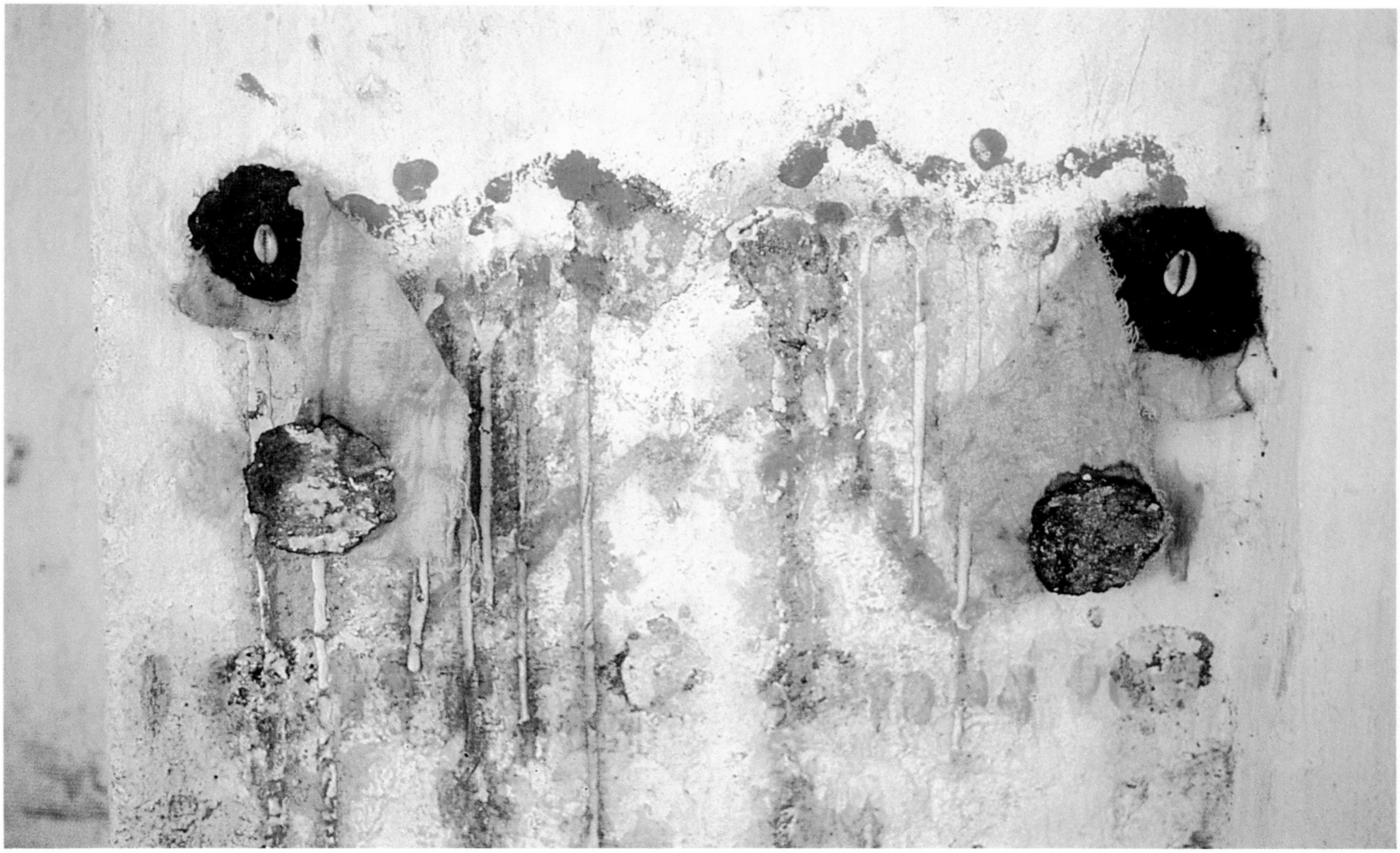

28 Mother Goddess figurine from Mohenjo-daro, *c.* 2500 BC. (Terracotta)

29 Mother and child figurine modelled by a village-woman of North Bengal. (Contemporary expression of traditional form. Terracotta)

30 Symbolic representation of a bride and bridegroom, drawn on a house-wall to ensure the happiness of the marriage. (Bakreswar Temple area, West Bengal)

Similarities in representation in images separated in time by more than three millennia suggest symbolic formulations owing less to tradition than to an archetype

31 Traditional marriage-proposal painting (*Kohbar*) made by a woman of Mithila in north Bihar State. (Contemporary expression of traditional form. Gouache on paper)

32 Libation jar with consecrated water and ritual flowers. (Kalighat, south Calcutta)

'The pot shows the universe.' – Bengali proverb

33 Ādivāsi (tribal) girls preparing clay for ritual pots. (Bastar, Madhya Pradesh)

34, 35 Ritual clay pots shaped according to surviving Vedic tradition, and used in the ancient Vedic fire altar ceremony, see plates 12–14. (Kerala)

36 The abundant waters of the Ganges, personified as the goddess Gaṅgā, and poured from ritual vessels by Śiva. (Himachal Pradesh, *c.* 18th century. Gouache on paper)

The goddess, her lotus symbol and her serpents

37 Lakshmī, goddess of fertility and wealth, with her flower, the lotus. (Bharhut, *c.* 2nd century BC. Stone)

38 Pitcher symbolizing Manasā, the serpent goddess (Barisal, Bangladesh. Contemporary expression of traditional form. Painted clay)

39 Yoni with vegetation issuing from it, painted on a house-wall. (Rajasthan. Contemporary expression of traditional form)

Plate 27
Calling upon goddesses, women all over India make paintings or drawings on mud floors or walls, known according to the region as *maṇḍana, raṅgoli, ālipanā,* and so on. They are drawn by means of a small piece of cloth wrapped round a finger, soaked in thin rice-paste. Such rice-paste drawings are particularly connected with certain rites called *Vratas* performed by girls and women, and their traditional designs have been handed down from mother to daughter over generations. The purpose of these rites is practical – to ensure prosperity and all other aspects of well-being. The drawing illustrated is an invocation to the Mother, Kālī.

Plates 28–29
Evidence of the ancient cult of the Mother is provided by a large number of terracotta figurines, dated *c.* 2500 BC, discovered in Harappa and Mohenjo-daro in the Indus Valley. They are crowned with an elaborate headdress and bedecked with ornaments, including necklaces and girdles around their hips. A contemporary mother and child modelled as a toy by a village-woman has similar symbolic attributes and testifies to an archetypal image.

Plate 30
Bride and bridegroom are represented in effigy by two pieces of cloth, traditionally supplied by the groom, while the painting in which these are used is made by the bride's family. Though the formal marriage ceremony varies considerably from region to region, there are certain rites common to many forms followed in India. Here, the bride and groom together take seven steps before the fire altar, each step representing a particular blessing. The marriage is complete with the taking of the seventh step. The man now places his hand over his wife's heart and says: 'Into my heart I take thy heart, thy mind shall follow my mind.' Finally the forehead of the bride is marked with the ritual vermilion dot, and water and flowers are sprinkled upon the heads of the couple.

Plate 31
Kohbar, the name for a Mithila woman's marriage-proposal drawing, offered to the man of her choice, is also the name for the room where the bride will receive her husband and where the couple will spend their first four nights of marriage. Mithila women's painting is in a highly distinctive traditional style, and like all traditional Indian art, is primarily religious in inspiration.

Plate 32
No ritual worship can start without the establishment of *ghaṭa*, the ceremonial jar of earthenware or metal, in front of the deity's pedestal. When the divinity underlying the universe is invited to descend into the sacred water contained in the vessel, the vessel becomes a powerful means of contact between the *sādhaka* (devotee) and the cosmos. The jar itself becomes a living entity by being ritually established (*ghaṭa sthāpana*) on a lump of clay forming a pedestal, or on a rice-paste drawing, or on a coloured-powder maṇḍala diagram. It is then consecrated with ritual ingredients and appropriate mantras. Very often, after the rites are completed the ghaṭa is allowed to remain undisturbed in the place of worship.

Plate 33
The preparation of ritual objects requires special procedures and disciplines. The *Ādivāsis*, the Indian tribal people, meticulously observe the traditional practices. Libation jars, for example, must be made with the right type of clay and be moulded and fired at auspicious times. The preparation, like ritual art itself, is deeply symbolic, and much of the significance of the observances is known only to initiates.

Plates 34–35
Ritual vessels of clay made for use in the Agnicayana (fire sacrifice) have been collected by Professor Frits Staal of the University of California. Their

traditional forms, like the ancient tradition of the Vedic fire sacrifice itself, have survived only in Kerala, and are likely soon to become extinct. The faithful preservation of the ritual of the preparation of the altar and its accessories 'remains one of the miracles of history'. The vessels are shaped with female breasts and an erect phallus between them. The phallus is consubstantial with the penetrating power of the universe; the breasts signify the feminine archetype as Mother Goddess and goddess of plenty.

Plate 36
India's most sacred river is personified as a goddess, Gaṅgā. The river poured down from the Himalayas as a mighty torrent that would have flooded the earth had not Śiva allowed it flow through his matted hair and so broken its fall. From the head of Śiva it flowed on as the 'seven streams'. Here, Śiva himself is performing ritual oblation, pouring Ganges water over his head from the sacred vessels.

Plate 37
The goddess of fertility and wealth is invoked as Lakshmī, the spouse of Vishṇu. She is said to have had several rebirths, in each one as the beloved of the Vishṇu-incarnation. When Vishṇu came as Rāma, Lakshmī was Sītā, when he came as Vāmana (dwarf), she was a lotus (Padmā). She is also worshipped as Kamalā, meaning 'lotus', symbolizing good fortune and prosperity.

The lotus belongs to this world and the world below and the world above; to earth, water and light. It enacts the transmutation from earth to air, from mud to perfume, from darkness to lustrous colour. Its shape points to all the directions of space; its openings and closings are the measure of time, of days and nights. It embraces all the elements and forms of the cosmos, while the pericarp refers to the mysteries of generation.

Plate 38
Images of the Great Mother, Mahāmāi, Śrī, Manasā, Ṣaṣṭhi or Śitalā, are found in all places. Manasā, the serpent goddess, is worshipped widely, both anthropomorphically and emblematically, although she is never represented as a serpent. The Manasā-ghaṭa is a pitcher symbolizing Manasā. 'Manas' signifies the power of the mind, and the goddess Manasā represents this power. As the serpent goddess, Manasā holds supreme sway over the powers of the serpent, both beneficial and malign.

Plate 39
The yantra of the goddess is the yoni or female triangle, representing at a simple level fertility and motherhood, at a deeper level the goddess as primal energy and as the genetrix of all things. Yoni is worshipped as the Ultimate Ground, the matrix from which arise the processes of creation, and into which all creation is in due time dissolved.

Ritual water vessel in the shape of the yoni

Chapter Four

Popular Cults

Local deities, guardians and protectors, *Grāma-devatās*, are at the heart of Indian village life, while side by side with these, a living language of signs expresses the hidden truths of customs and beliefs. Such communications may even be opposed to formal doctrine, and they are open to all to read.

Indian popular art owes its vividness and richness to the Sanskritic heritage combined with living tradition. Myths and legends are humanized, and their messages are applied to the present time and place. Yet the essential unity of worship is not lost amid all the diversity. There is plenty of room for freedom of thought, while the underlying purpose of ritual remains everywhere the same.

Popular ritual art reflects a keen sense of the natural order, and represents it in a way adapted to human understanding. To the people of India, the levels of being are a present reality, and the ritual act simply allows the worshipper to become more aware of the integration of the self in a wider world-order. The human sense of isolation is overcome in a variety of observances. Ritual bathing, the festival lighting of lamps and so on, all point to the mysteries underlying existence.

In the countryside, nothing is seen as too low or too high to be reached by worship. People look to symbols and signs, images and myths, to solve the daily problems of living, as well as for spiritual nourishment. Ritual art touches every aspect of life, and every village is ready to maintain elaborate rites and ceremonies.

Local myths, legends and art-forms have harmonized the unknowable and the known in a relationship so close and intuitive that the difference between god and the world ceases to exist. This identification does not depend on any doctrine, but on involvement of all the senses, and on the arousing of particular kinds of emotions and aspirations in the hearts and minds of the worshippers.

. . . it's not the road you walk, it is the walking.

VATSYAYANA

Shapes and colours on village and household shrines are not arbitrary, but are concentrations of meaning, a language of the symbolic life of daily worship

PREVIOUS PAGE
40 Doors of a Bhil Ādivāsi (tribal) Kālī temple. (Rajasthan, traditional form)

41 The monkey-god Hanumān-ji. (Banaras, stone. Contemporary expression of traditional form)

42, 43 Grāma-devatās, village deities. (Rajasthan, stone; West Bengal, plaster and brick. Contemporary expressions of traditional form)

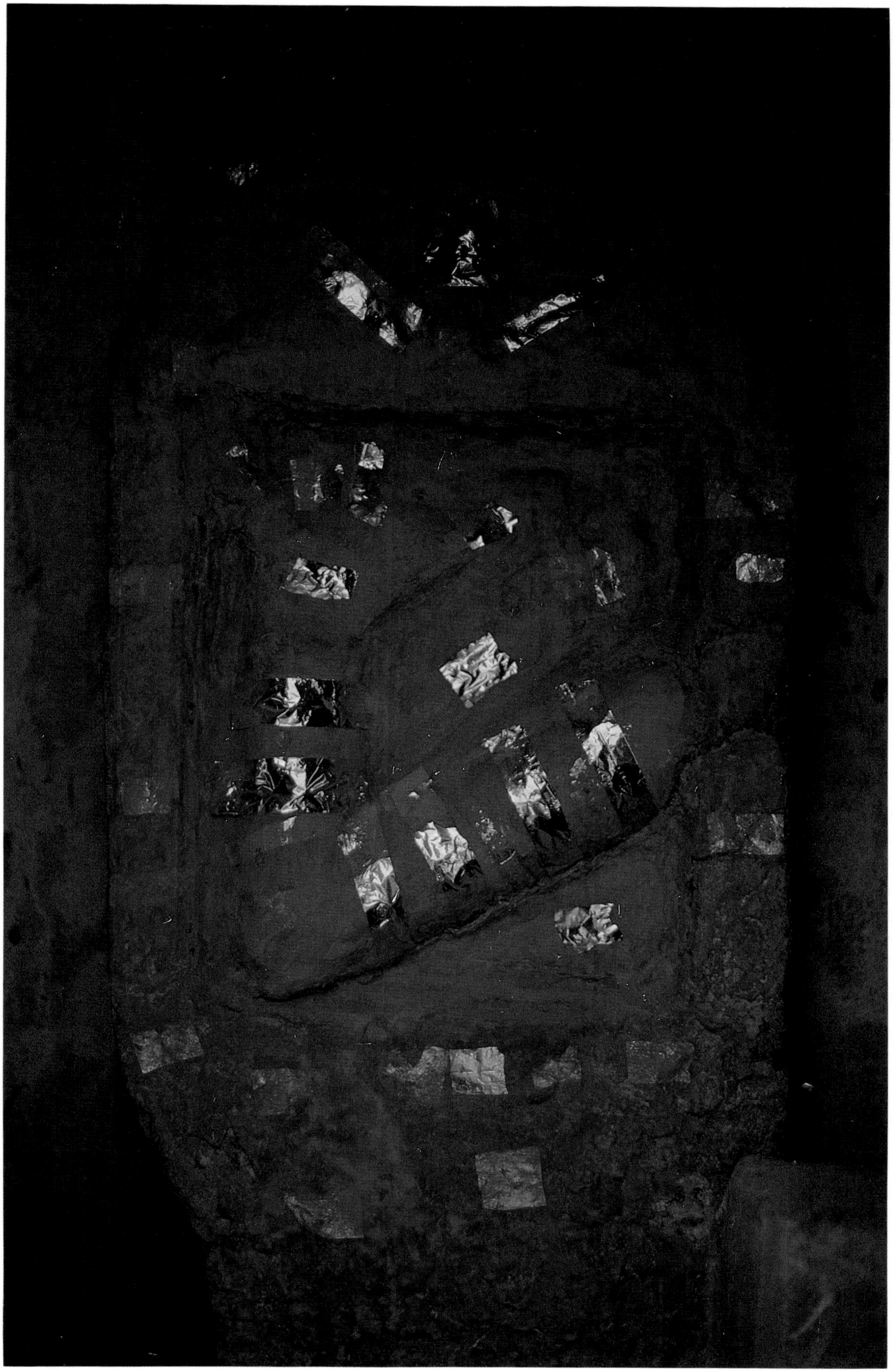

44 Corner with a household shrine. (Rajasthan)

45 Shrine of a Harijan mud hut. (Rajasthan)

Auspicious colours mark the places where rites are performed for special purposes. The offerings may be very simple or very elaborate

46–48 Mānat, a pledge intended to draw the attention of the deity to one's desires. (Jejuri, Maharashtra. Vermilion-coloured tree, below right; painted wall-shrine, opposite)

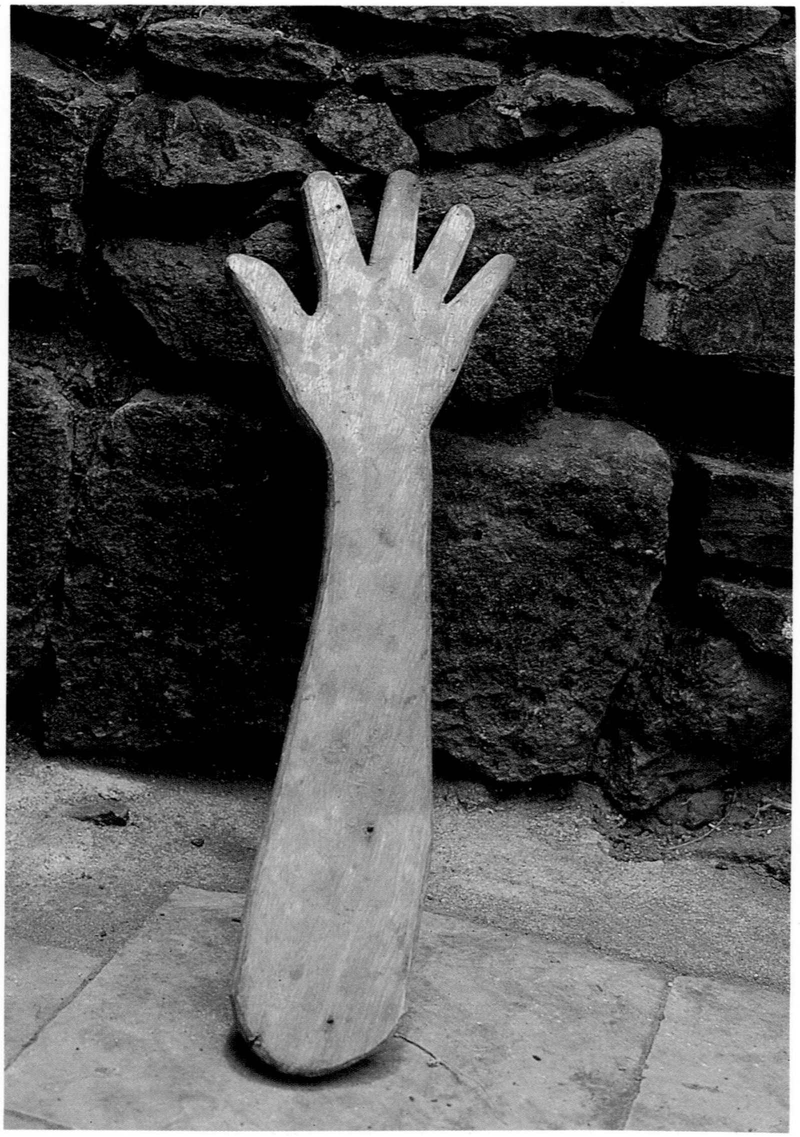

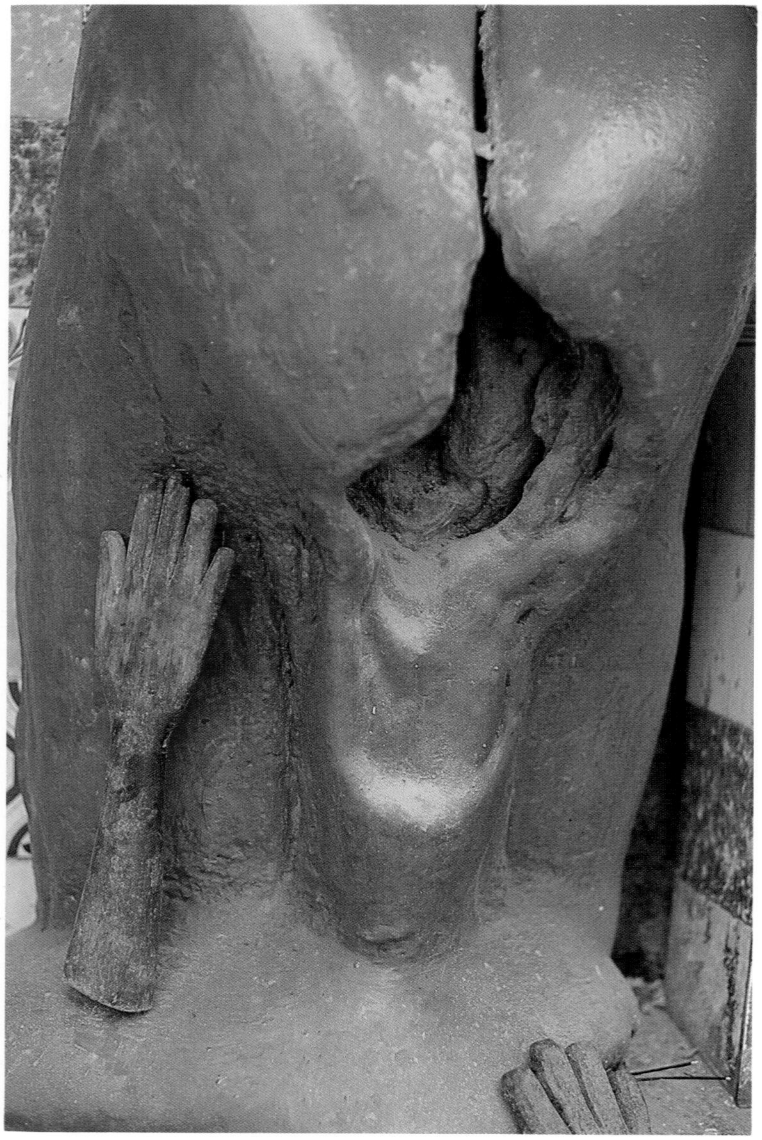

For the Festival of Lights, auspicious yantra diagrams are drawn by women, and on the first day the windows are kept open to welcome the goddesses Lakshmī and Pārvatī into the house

49 Kolam on the courtyard floor. (Pondicherry, contemporary expression of traditional form. Rice-paste and earth pigment)

50 Auspicious drawings for the Festival. (Bhopal, Madhya Pradesh, contemporary expression of traditional form)

51 Divālī, the Festival of Lights, one of the most important and spectacular popular festivals

The deity is invoked to enter the dreaming mind of the pilgrim

52 Devotee prostrating herself in the Dream Ritual at the Śiva temple of Tārakesvara, West Bengal

Plate 40
The entrance to a shrine is sacred, and so is the threshold, for it marks the division between the sacred and the profane world. One must enter a temple-doorway with reverence, making ritual offerings to the threshold before entering the dwelling-place where the deity is installed. The symbolic colours of the doorway prepare the mind of the worshipper for the approach to the divine.

Plate 41
Sacred eyes watchful, vermilion-smeared and profusely garlanded by worshippers, the monkey-god Hanumān-ji is the bestower of boons on every passer-by.

Plates 42–43
The icons of local deities, *Grāma-devatās*, are the focus of village ritual. Coloured with vermilion paste and ornamented with golden leaf, they have metal eyes to express their overwhelming energy and their ceaseless vigilance for their people.

Plates 44–45
C.G. Jung has said that man's most vital need is to discover his own reality through the cultivation of a symbolic life. 'Have you got a corner somewhere in your houses where you perform rites, such as you can see in India?' No household in India lacks a secluded corner where daily worship is performed, either publicly or in privacy, by the members of the household for their spiritual progress.

The entrance to the inner small chamber of a Harijan household shrine is one symbolic step above earth level. In keeping with the inward-outward correspondence, one ascends to enter the sanctuary.

Plates 46–48
The *mānat* or pledge is offered to mark an important event in daily life, or to obtain a personal desire. There is a period of preparatory fasting, and ritual consecration involving a special type of worship, in which *pārthanā*, 'supplication', is offered to the deity.

Plate 49
The making of ritual drawings known variously as *kolam*, *ālipanā*, etc., is widespread in South India. They are drawn to record a vow, or on an auspicious occasion such as the Festival of Lights. They are generally painted by women, and usually on the mud floor of the courtyard. Most of the diagrams are square or circular, and have cosmogonic significance.

Plate 50–51
The popular festival of Divālī is also known by its Sanskrit name, Dipāvalī, which means 'a row of lights'. It lasts for five days and nights in October-November (Āswin-Kārtik), from the dark half of the first month to the light half of second. The fourth, darkest night, is Divālī proper, when thousands of earthenware bowls filled with oil are lighted in the evening and set up in rows inside and outside the house. It is as if the whole of India were alight with lamps and fireworks. The first day is generally dedicated to the worship of the goddesses Lakshmī and Pārvatī and windows are kept open to welcome them into the house. The following days are observed as the worship of the goddess Kālī, specially in Bengal. Throughout the day there is fasting, bathing, and ritual preparation for the midnight worship. Diagrams (known as *āripana* in Bihar, *ālipanā* in Bengal, *osa* in Orissa, *chowka* in Uttar Pradesh, *maṇḍana* in Rajasthan, *sathia* in Gujarat, *raṅgoli* in Maharashtra and *kolam* in Tamil Nadu and throughout South India) are drawn on the floor near the threshold and in the courtyards of houses, as auspicious signs.

Plate 52
For centuries, thousands of pilgrims have gathered at the Śiva-liṅga Temple of Tārakesvara (Lord as Saviour). Devotees approach the temple by repeatedly prostrating themselves along the way, and then lie flat under a white cloth in the temple courtyard to await the Dream Vision that will reveal to them all that they desire to know.

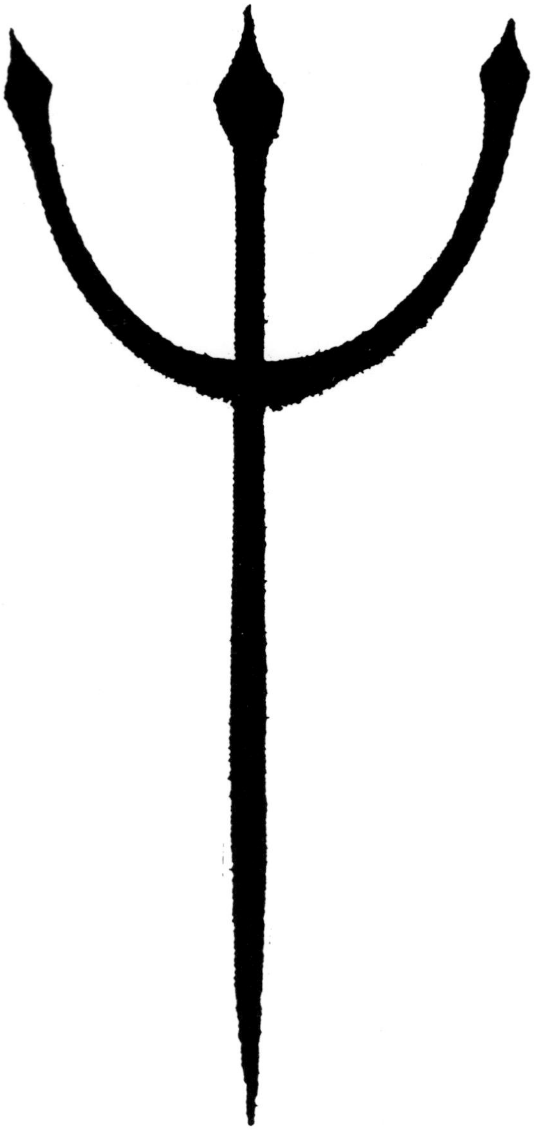

Chapter Five

Śivaism

Śiva is the Absolute. From very early times, from Kashmir to Kanyakumari and beyond, he has been worshipped as supreme. A living god, he is the Great Yogi, the Supreme Mendicant, the King of Dancers, the Lover, the Bridegroom, the Husband.

Over the course of time Śivaism has taken different forms in different regions. Vīra-Śaiva in the Karnataka, Śaiva-Siddhānta in Tamil Nadu and Advaita Śaivism in Kashmir are the three main branches. Vīra-Śaiva or Liṅgāyat is the name of the Śaiva sect which believes that there is a Being who is called Śiva-tattva. In his creation aspect, by the activation of his inherent energy (Śakti), this Being becomes two: Liṅga (Śiva as liṅga) for worship, and Aṅga the individual soul, the worshipper. The Śaiva-Siddhānta doctrine grew out of the mystical writings of the Ālvārs from the seventh century onwards, giving rise to a cult marked by intense devotional fervour. Kashmir Śaivism, or the Trika system, dating from the beginning of the ninth century, developed a highly intellectual monistic theory. The system regards the Supreme Reality, Śiva, as unitary and Pure Consciousness, conscious of itself through reflection which is identified with Śakti. Śiva-Śakti, a bi-unity, contain the potential of all that is ever likely to be.

The Śaiva philosophy, as Jaidev Singh indicates (*Pratyabhijñahṛdayam*), conceives of the Supreme as artist. Just as an artist cannot contain his joy within himself, but pours it out in a song, a painting or a poem, so the Supreme Artist pours out his splendour in manifestation or creation. The force is not blind, whether in creation or dissolution; the Ultimate Reality is Universal Consciousness as well as Universal Energy or Power, manifested in five aspects: consciousness, bliss, desire, knowledge and activity. These five aspects are symbolized as Śiva's five faces. Śiva is both transcendental and immanent.

If the Highest Reality [Parama Śiva] did not manifest in infinite variety, but remained within its solid singleness, it would neither be the Highest Power nor Consciousness, but something like a jar.

ABHINAVAGUPTA, TANTRĀLOKA

PREVIOUS PAGE

53 Ice-liṅga, symbol of Śiva. (Amarnath cave, Kashmir)

54 Śiva's trident wrapped in a ritual red cloth representing the feminine energy. (Temple interior, Tamil Nadu. Contemporary expression of traditional form)

55 A Śaivite, or follower of Śiva, annointed and preparing sandalwood paste for the performance of ritual worship. (Tamil Nadu)

56 Earth pigment used for painting ritual images. (Kumartuli, north Calcutta)

Śiva's creative power, the feminine energy (śakti), is awakened during yogic meditation to rise through the body's three subtle channels, symbolized by the trident. The feminine energy is represented by the scarlet cloth enfolding the trident, and also by the ritual marks on the body of the devotee

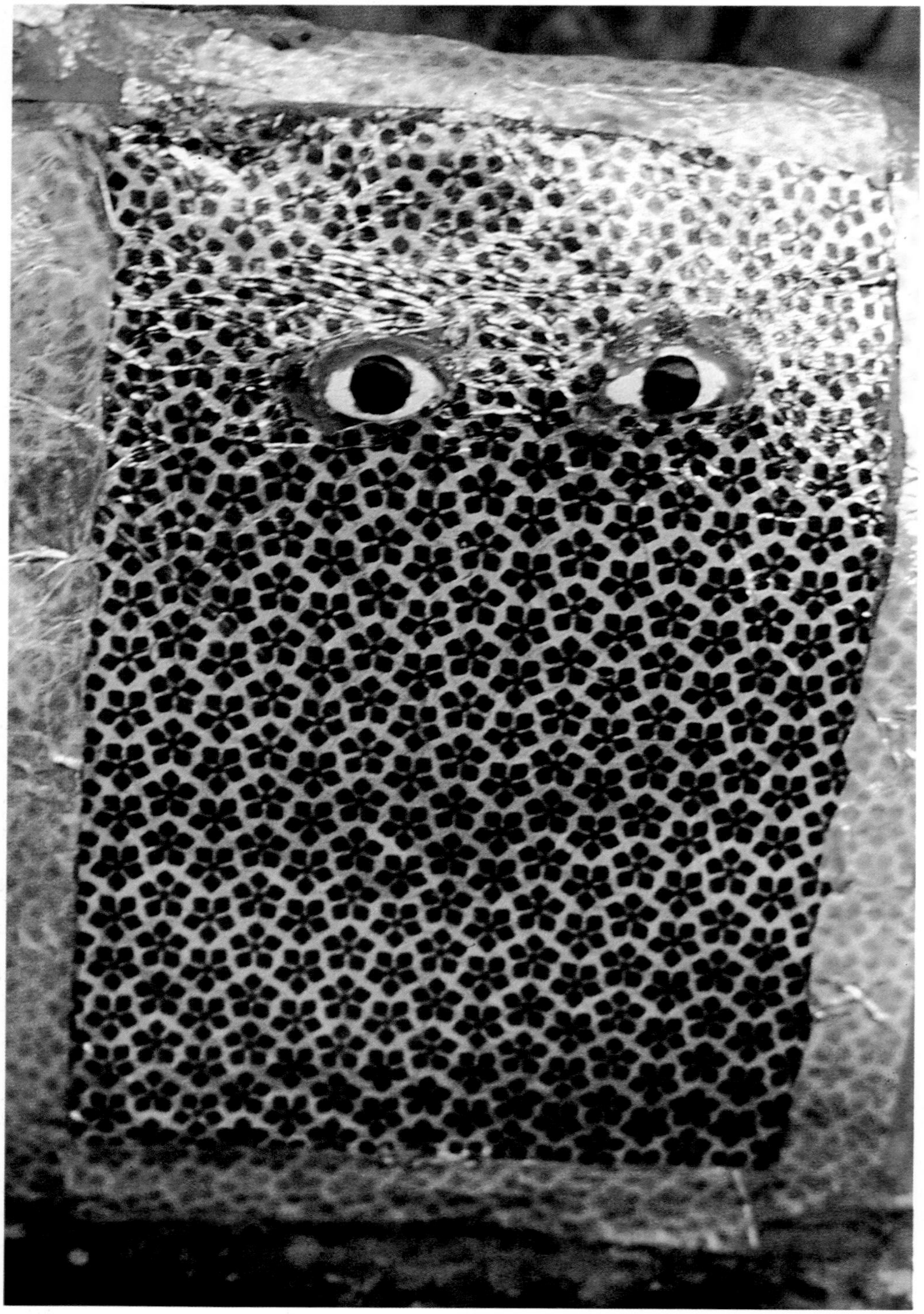

58, 59 Wayside shrines of Śiva, left, in his Terrible aspect as Bhairava, and opposite, incorporating his emblem, the trident. (Contemporary expressions of traditional form. Left, Rajasthan, printed paper and metal eyes, on stone. Right, Poona, paper and cloth on stone)

Painted stones and wayside shrines remind the passer-by of the terrors of the unknown, and of destruction

57 Bhairava, a Terrible aspect of Śiva. (New Delhi. Stone)

60, 61 Evening worship before the Śiva-liṅga by the priests of Visvanātha Temple, Banaras

62 Mask of Śiva Bhairava. (Udaipur, Rajasthan, *c.* 18th century. Brass)

Each utensil used for temple rites has symbolic meaning, and contributes to the awareness of the worshipper. A Śiva-mask covers the Śiva-liṅga during public worship

Offerings are made to the Śiva-liṅga, representing the substance of the universe in formation and dissolution, and to the liṅga-yoni, symbolizing the two antithetical principles whose 'synthesis' restores perfect equilibrium and continuity

63 Śiva-liṅga. (Kalighat, south Calcutta. Contemporary expression of traditional form. Stone)

64 Śivaliṅga-yoni, representing the union of the male and female principles. (Banaras. Contemporary expression of traditional form. Stone)

OVERLEAF

65 Liṅga of colourless, translucent rock-crystal. (Nepal, *c.* 17th century)

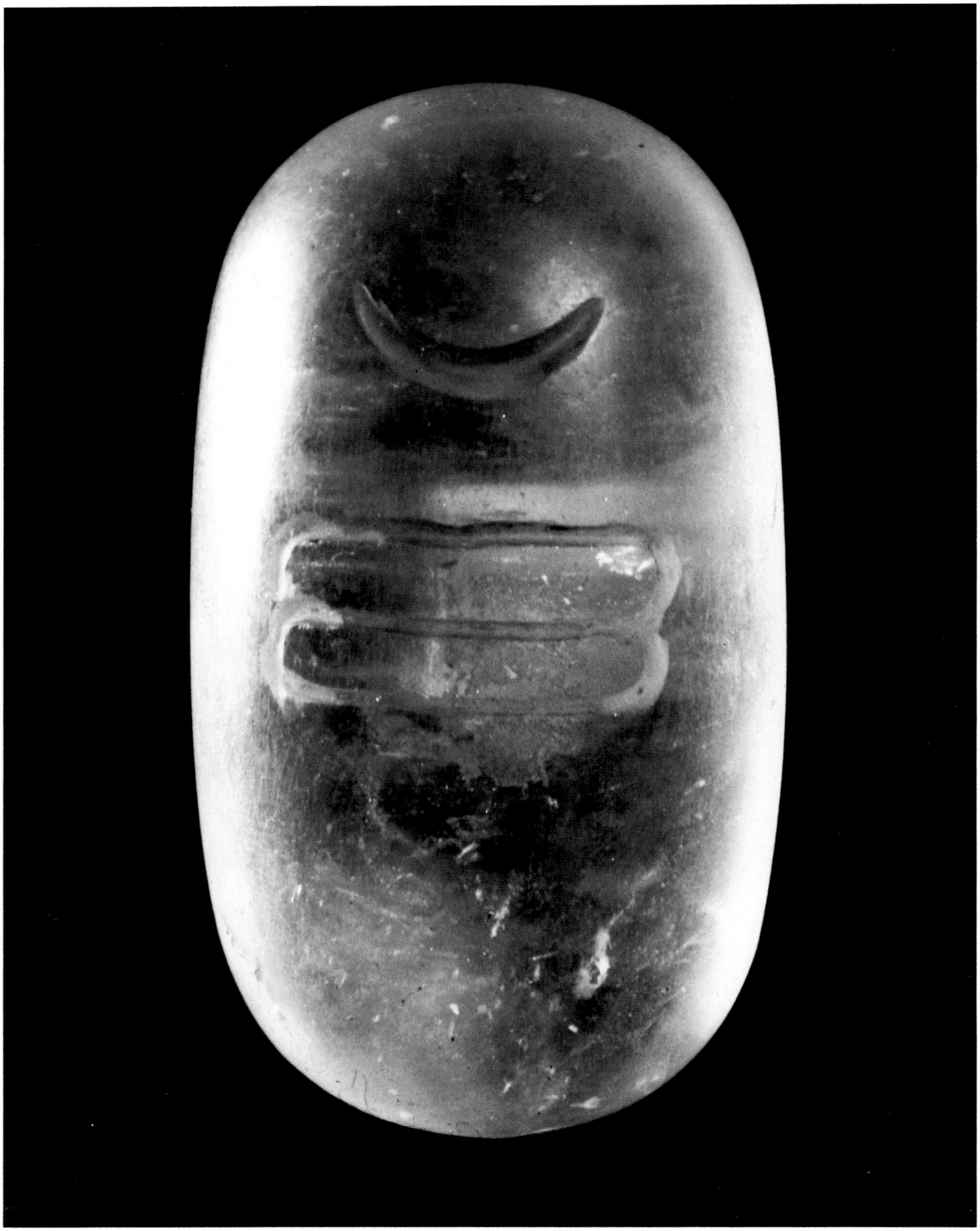

Plate 53
The liṅga-shaped ice block has been formed in a cave high in the Himalayas by water dripping from the mountain roof. It is believed that the ice-image grows every lunar month during the bright half, and partly melts away in the dark half. This sacred place of pilgrimage was discovered many hundreds of years ago by yogis who recognized in the natural ice pillar the symbol of Śiva. Every year, thousands of pilgrims climb the difficult path to Amarnath cave at 13,000 feet to perform ritual worship there.

Plate 54
The trident (*trisūla*) of Śiva represents creation, preservation and dissolution. It also refers to the three subtle channels of the human body, Idā, Piṅgalā and Sushumnā. Through these subtle channels, according to tantra-yoga, Kuṇḍalinī Śakti, the cosmic feminine energy, ascends from the root-centre Mūlādhāra at the base of the spine to reach Sahasrāra at the crown of the head. Śakti as female energy and as the creative power of Śiva is represented in this temple icon by the ceremonial red cloth and the fruit at the top. The trident represents the source of everything, the origin of the phenomenal world, as well as the conscious plan of creation and the principle of knowledge or consciousness.

Plate 55
The Śaivite devotee's body is annointed with sandalwood paste in preparation for the rite of worship. Such ceremonial worship may involve no more than simple daily offerings of flowers, water, etc., either at home or in the temple. The ritual marks are regarded as cosmic cross-points, since the body is considered an expression of one's psyche. In yogic meditation the body becomes the chief instrument of worship.

Plate 56
Five pigments – white (*sveta*), yellow (*pīta*), lampblack (*kṛishṇa*), green-brown (*haritāla*) and red (*rakta*) – are employed by the traditional artist in the painting of images. Gold leaf and gold-dust, silver leaf and silver-dust, may also be employed. In the preparation of the paints the seeds of the Tentul tree (tamarind) are boiled to give a paste into which the colours are mixed. Barley-paste may also be used. The artists are adepts in the mixing of these colours, which retain their brilliance for long periods.

Plates 57–58
Śiva in his Terrible aspect of Bhairava (and his consort Śakti in her Terrible aspect of Bhairavī) represent universal dissolution. A painted stone or a mountain rock-shrine remind the passer-by of the terrors of the unknown and of destruction. Bhairava is the name of a classical *rāga* performed by a male singer at dawn in August-September (Bhādra-Āswin), arousing in the listeners feelings of awe, terror and reverence. It concerns 'Śiva in ascetic aspect, with matted locks, besmeared with ashes, and adorned with skulls'. A feminine form of the *rāga* known as Bhairavī is sung at dusk during the same season.

Plate 59
Śiva's trident has been painted on a stone set up beneath a tree. Cloth and cotton threads are criss-crossed to create *laya*, absorption or dissolution points. The figure created by the threads is incessantly in motion. Only in motion can the cross-points preserve their power and generate their rhythms – the vibrations or vital energies that sustain form.

Plates 60–61
The Śiva-liṅga is worshipped in the Visvanātha Temple by the moving of lighted lamps (*dīpa*) in a clockwise direction, accompanied by the chanting of mantras and the sounding of gongs and bells. Homage is paid to the icon with lights, sounds, flowers, and other offerings. Utensils for ritual

worship are made either of earthenware or of pure metals, generally copper, brass, gold, or silver. Copper is considered to be the purest of all metals. Particularly important aesthetically are ornamental copper plates (*pushpapātras*) of different sizes, used for presenting flowers and other offerings. Bells (*ghaṅṭās*) may have handle-decorations of foliage or linear devices and a bird-finial. Tray-stands may be in the shape of a boldly modelled bull or peacock. Copper water stoups (*koṣa* and *kuṣi*) are used everywhere for the consecrated water, and symbolize the male and female principles. Ritual lamps (*pañcha-pradīpas*) are of infinite variety. The most striking are standing lamps in the form of a female holding five shallow bowls which are used as oil lamps.

Plate 62
The liṅga-icon is covered by a mask which is removed by a priest at the time of consecration with water and libations, and replaced for public worship. Rituals are performed by priests on behalf of the community, often in the presence of devotees. Hymns are recited in front of the image, then the priest addresses the divine by means of sacred mantras and symbolic hand-gestures. The deity is awakened, and due attention is paid to the divine presence with the consecration of vessels and ingredients, the bathing and dressing of the sacred image and the offering of foods. The image is annointed with oils, camphor and sandalwood, is garlanded and entertained with moving lights and flowers.

Plate 63
The liṅga, according to the *Skanda Purāṇa*, symbolizes the substance of the universe in the process of formation and dissolution. It also signifies the static principle, which has been represented in the shape of an egg (*aṇḍa-rūpa*), when it characterizes Śiva in the 'attributeless' (*nishkala*) aspect.

Plate 64
The union of Śiva and his Energy, Śakti, is symbolized by the combined form of liṅga-yoni. Duality appears with the first vibration in the undifferentiated substratum. Taking the form of poles of attraction, it becomes manifested in the whole of creation as male and female characteristics. There can be no creation without the relation of opposites. There can be no creation from Śiva alone or from Nature (Prakṛiti) alone: the union of enjoyer and enjoyed, of a passive and an active principle, is essential. Yoni (Śakti) as energy quanta or power of manifestation is represented as a circle. The liṅga is then the Bindu, the circle's invisible central point. In manifestation, liṅga and yoni become distinct entities. The yoni-circle is transformed into the yoni-triangle, the Creative Ground. The liṅga-yoni image represents the union of antithetical principles. It is a synthesis that restores balance, changing a state of chaos caused by separation into perfect continuity and equilibrium.

Plate 65
The 'formless' is represented by many symbols, including ether, a pillar of light, the Universal Egg, and, as here, by a liṅga of translucent, colourless rock-crystal, marked with the Śiva emblem of two parallel lines and a crescent moon.

Chapter Six

Vishṇuism

In the Hindu creation myth, Vishṇu is the principle which maintains the balance between the life-processes of the universe and the negative and disruptive forces. In the *Purāṇas* Vishṇu is referred to as Nārāyaṇa, the all-pervading cohesive force, associated with the primeval waters. He is represented as reclining on the thousand-hooded serpent Śesha in yogic trance-sleep. Brahmā, the creator, is seated on a lotus that springs from the navel of Vishṇu. Vishṇu's unconscious energies, symbolized by the umbilical cord, are not detached but always linked with manifestation or creation through Brahmā.

His role as 'preserver' explains Vishṇu's incarnations to redeem humankind. His avatāras, 'descents', are usually ten in number: the creatures fish, tortoise, boar, man-lion, dwarf, and the sages and divine beings Paraśurāma, Rāma, Buddha, Kalki (a future incarnation who will come on horseback), and, most important of all, Kṛishṇa.

Kṛishṇa's legends answer many deep social and spiritual needs. Love is the vital force of Vishṇuism. *Bhakti*, fervent devotion to a personal god, is one of the paths to liberation. In its essence, *bhakti* is a close relationship, a deep attachment to a personal god, and intense love and supreme longing for him. It also implies total self-surrender, and the devotee is free to communicate with Kṛishṇa without reserve. Kṛishṇa may be a friend, a colleague, a child, a lover: he can be communicated with in the same way whether in the home or the temple.

The daily worship of Kṛishṇa involves elaborate rituals. More than sixteen ritual acts in succession are performed for Kṛishṇa under his names of Śrī Nāth-ji of Nathadwara, Baṅkubihāri of Vrindavana and Jagannātha of Puri. The devotion induced is not filial, but the love between the beloved and the lover, as exemplified in the eternal love of Rādhā and Kṛishṇa. It is the universal human emotion in which self is transcended, and two become as one.

Caitanya	*What is the goal of life?*
Disciple	*A man must follow the rules and injunctions prescribed in the scriptures.*
Caitanya	*This is the external part of religion – only a means, not the goal. Try again.*
Disciple	*Surrendering the fruits of action to Kṛishṇa.*
Caitanya	*This, too, is external. Try again.*
Disciple	*Realizing the devotion that arises from self-surrender.*
Caitanya	*This, too, is external. Try again.*
Disciple	*Realizing with knowledge.*
Caitanya	*This too, is external. Try again.*
Disciple	*Realizing pure devotion, which knows no reason.*
Caitanya	*That is good. Go further.*
Disciple	*Acquiring the spirit of service to Kṛishṇa.*
Caitanya	*That is good. Go further.*
Disciple	*To love Kṛishṇa as a friend.*
Caitanya	*That is very good. Go further.*
Disciple	*To love Kṛishṇa as a child.*
Caitanya	*That is also good. Go further.*
Disciple	*To love Kṛishṇa as the beloved bridegroom.*
Caitanya	*This is no doubt the goal. But tell me if there is any attainment further than this.*
Disciple	*My understanding does not reach beyond this. But there is another stage called Prem-Vilās-Vivarta.*

The biographers of Śrī Caitanya record that at this point Śrī Caitanya stopped Ramananda (one of his principal disciples) from speaking, indicating thereby that the highest truth, the highest secret, must not be divulged. Prem-Vilās-Vivarta is the truth of mystic union, wherein there is no longer a distinction between the lover and the beloved. In this is realized the truth of nondualism: Tat Tvam asi – Thou art That.

PREVIOUS PAGE
66 Kṛishṇa and Rādhā – the language of human desire and love. (Jaipur school, *c.* 1810. Gouache on paper)

67 Vishṇu reclining on the primordial serpent-power. (Kangra school, *c.* 18th century. Gouache on paper)

68 Incarnation of Vishṇu as Kūrma-avatāra, the Tortoise incarnation. (Kalighat school, south Calcutta, *c.* 19th century. Gouache on paper)

69 Śrī Nāth-ji, a form of Krishṇa, adorned for worship. (Rajasthan, *c.* 19th century. Gouache on paper)

Among Vishṇu's many incarnations it is the god Kṛishṇa to whom a fervent devotion is directed

70 Jagannātha, Lord of the Universe, a form of Kṛishṇa widely worshipped in Orissa and Bengal. (Traditional form. Laquer on cloth)

71 Āratī, evening worship with a moving light

72 Govinda-ji, the form of Kṛishṇa worshipped in the Maharaja's Palace Temple at Jaipur. (*c.* 17th century. Stone)

Emblems of all that we perceive in the universe, all that is made use of by us, should be offered to the chosen deity. Thrice-daily rites of Kṛishṇa and Rādhā include their ceremonious awakening, their ritual bathing and annointing, their dressing in robes and ornaments according to the hour, the day and the season, their invocation and adoration, surrender and salutation with offerings, the waving of a lighted lamp to the sound of mantras and devotional songs, and lastly, the distribution of offerings, before the deity is bidden farewell to sleep

73 Evening worship of Govinda-ji. (Temple of Govinda-ji, Jaipur)

74 Rādhā, chief of the milkmaids or gopīs, worshipped at the Jaipur Maharaja's Palace Temple of Govinda-ji. (*c.* 17th century. Stone)

75 Kṛishṇa-image and pilgrims' saris in a tree near the Yamuna River, at the pilgrim centre of Vrindavan in northern India

The 'stealing of the clothes', an episode in which the gopīs' nakedness before Kṛishṇa is a metaphor for transcendental union and the realization of pure joy (ānanda)

76 Vastra-haraṇ, 'the stealing of the clothes'. Kṛishṇa steals the gopīs saris while they are bathing in the Yamuna River. (Kalighat school, south Calcutta, *c.* 19th century. Gouache on paper)

Kṛishṇa's upbringing among cowherds is recalled in a painted cloth wall-hanging of his shrine, of which a number of sets provide backgrounds for different occasions, and also in miniature versions made by temple painters to be taken home by pilgrims. Like the Kalighat Temple painting of Hanumān, Rāma and Sītā (plate 80), these miniatures help to intensify the worshippers' sense of tender personal devotion to the divinity

77 Gopashtami, the Festival of Cattle. (Rajasthan, *c.* 1830. Gouache on cloth)

78 Vaishṇavite of South India with the tilaka-mark on his forehead

79 The tilaka, Vaishṇavite ritual mark, painted on a temple wall. (South India. Contemporary)

80 The monkey-god Hanumān reveals the shrine of Sītā and Rāma in his breast. (Kalighat school, south Calcutta. *c.* 1850. Gouache on paper)

Plate 66
The Kṛishṇa and Rādhā theme distils the essense of a culture. The warm sensuous humanity of Vishṇuism has found expression in poetry, and especially in painting, of the utmost beauty. The female beauty, the *hlādinī-śakti*, Rādhā, personifies the beauty of the cosmos. There is a loving interest in landscape, the countryside, rivers, trees, birds, cattle and flowers. Love is expressed as a profound natural tenderness and solicitude, a serene joy based upon dedication and communion between the souls of man and woman. The union of Rādhā and Kṛishṇa signifies the union of Soul with the Absolute.

Plate 67
Vishṇu, the Preserver, reclining on the primordial serpent-power, Śesha, symbolizes the Supreme Being in a state of cosmic slumber. On the umbilical lotus is seated Brahmā, the Creator, encountering the destructive forces in the chaotic waters of the dissolved cosmos.

Plate 68
Vishṇu's incarnations range from fish to tortoise to man to deity. In India it has always been held that no gulf of kind exists between the various forms of existence.

Plate 69
The most famous image of Kṛishṇa as Śrī Nāth-ji is in Nathadwara, twenty miles north of Udaipur. He is shown in evening robes.

Plate 70
Jagannātha (Kṛishṇa) is worshipped at Puri in Orissa in the medieval Jagannātha Temple. The tower of the main temple, which rises to a height of two hundred feet, contains the sacred image of Jagannātha with Balabhadra (Balarāma), the brother, and Subhadrā, the sister of Kṛishṇa. Thousands of pilgrims travel to Puri from all parts of India, especialy during the two great annual festivals. One is for the images' ritual bath, the other when they are carried in a great procession through the town during the eight-day Rathajātrā Festival, starting on the second day of the bright fortnight of Ashāḍha (June-July). The richly decorated sixteen-wheeled wooden chariot (*ratha*) of Jagannātha (hence 'juggernaut') is drawn through the streets by professional pullers and pilgrims. *Chitrakaras* (painters) around the temple area provide large as well as miniature paintings on cloth, known as *puri patas*, depicting episodes of Jagannātha's life.

Plate 71
A distinction is made between those rites that are *nitya* or obligatory, and those that are *kāmya* or optional. The nightly deity-worship, āratī, is an obligatory rite, performed with lights, flowers and colours.

Plates 72–73
Govinda-ji (a name of Kṛishṇa) is awakened at dawn, bathed and annointed with sandalwood paste, adorned with fresh robes and ornaments. Then follow invocation and adoration of the deity; surrender and salutation with garlands and flowers, offerings of food and other ritual ingredients, and circumambulation, the ceremony in which the devotee walks around the icon or the shrine in which the icon is housed. The *upācāras*, rites of an installed deity, make use of outward, physical ingredients to represent the senses and subtle elements. All that we perceive in the whole universe, all that is made use of by us, should be offered to the *ishṭa-devatā*, the chosen deity. The rites must include *āratī*, the 'waving' of a lighted lamp before the image, generally in a clockwise direction, accompanied by chanting of mantras and singing of devotional songs, and end with the distribution of *prasāda*, the offerings of food, to the devotees. Ceremonies take place in the morning, afternoon and evening, before the deity is finally bidden farewell, enshrined on a portable altar. Ritual manuals decree the robes and ornaments of the

deities which vary according to season, hour, and occasion.

Plate 74
Rādhā, the chief of the *gopīs* (cowgirls, milkmaids) and favourite consort of Kṛishṇa, is worshipped as the beauty of the world. The power of bliss which she represents is the very essence of Kṛishṇa. In later legends she is described as the incarnation of the goddess Lakshmī. Another story recounts that Kṛishṇa became two: one 'half' male, the other 'half' female. Rādhā became the symbol of perfect devotion, and by the thirteenth century, was worshipped alongside Kṛishṇa. The Rādhā-Kṛishṇa cult, which celebrates the divine and sacred love between the pair, is widespread, especially in north India, Gujarat and Bengal.

Plate 75
Vastra-haraṇ, 'the stealing of the clothes', is recalled in the ritual of throwing saris and other garments up to an image of Kṛishṇa installed on a branch of the Kadamba tree by women going to the Yamuna River for ritual bathes.

Plate 76
The milkmaids, *gopīs*, decide to bathe in the river in the month of Agrahāyana (November-December), an auspicious time to seek a boon from the goddess Gaurī. The boon they desire is the love of Kṛishṇa, Lord of the gopīs. Kṛishṇa, who is grazing his herds nearby, steals their clothing while they are in the water. A search follows. When they find Kṛishṇa sitting with the clothing in a Kadamba tree, they immediately conceal their bodies beneath the water. He demands that they come out one by one to retrieve their garments. The gopīs are angry, but eventually they comply, and promise to return to sport with him in the following New Year. Abandoning all concealment and standing naked, face to face, is a metaphor for self-surrender and the primal state of oneness.

Plate 77
Śrī Nāth-ji surrounded by cows and cowherds is a reference to Kṛishṇa's early playground, called Golaka, 'cow-place'. The painters of Nathadwara Temple provide hangings for the shrine, and also small paintings on paper, such as this, for use in ritual worship in the temple, or in pilgrims' household shrines.

Plate 78–9
The *tilaka*, also called *ṭīkā*, is a ritual mark made on the forehead, arms or chest, with red, yellow or white pigment, with *sindūra* (vermilion), sandalwood paste or ashes, to designate one's sect. The marks may be horizontal or perpendicular lines, dots, rectangles, circles, oblongs or triangles.

The mark of the followers of Vishṇu, Kṛishṇa or Rāma is generally perpendicular, and includes a centre line with a stroke on either side, sometimes with a dot in the middle, denoting the footprint of Vishṇu.

Plate 80
Rāma said to Hanumān: 'In what light do you see me?' Hanumān replied: 'Rāma, when I have sense of ego left in me I see that thou art the whole and I am the part, thou art the master, I am the servant; but when I attain the highest knowledge I see that thou art myself and I am thee . . .' (parable of Ramakrishna). Hanumān the monkey-god opens his breast to reveal that Sītā and Rāma are always in his heart, signifying the identity of the inner self (Ātman) with the Universal Self (Brahman), the Ultimate Reality, the One. Such paintings of the characters in the *Rāmāyaṇa* and other epics are made by folk artists known as *Patuās* who crowd round the Kalighat Temple, south Calcutta.

Chapter Seven

Śaktism

Female divinities play a most significant role in Hindu mythology and ritual. Their importance grew steadily from the post-Vedic period onwards, until in Tantra and Śākta, which take their names from writings known respectively as *Tantras* or *Śāktāgamas*, the female power dominates, and the gods are virtually relegated to second place.

In cults which elevate the feminine principle above the masculine, the many and various goddesses become, in effect, facets of the one feminine principle, personified as Śakti or Devī, the energizing force that vitalizes the masculine principle, which is dormant – even dead – without her.

Thus in the *Mārkaṇḍeya Purāṇa* (*c.* 400 AD) the manifestation of the goddess Durgā is described as being in order to overthrow demonic force, the demons or *asuras* against whom the great gods are powerless. The mantras that are chanted during the Durgā-pūjā festival tell how, again and again, the demons triumphed and the gods were prevented from exercising their celestial functions. In the crisis, the goddess appeared to save the world from the suffering that is the consequence of unbalanced power.

The goddess Kālī is said to have been born from the brow of Durgā during the battle with the demons. The image of Kālī for worship is as the annihilating power of Time (Kāla) and as the energy of creation and dissolution.

Innumerable pilgrim-places have been dedicated to goddesses. Cape Comorin, at the southernmost tip of India, is named for 'Kanyā-kumāri', 'young virgin', and the goddess is worshipped there with elaborate rituals in the Kanyā-kumāri Temple.

Each of the goddesses has a specific cosmic function: each holds the key to the transpersonal experience of the seeker. The śaktis represent the dynamic unity of existence, in which all aspects of life have been fused to form a whole.

Thou art formless, though possessing form, for by means of Māyā Thou dost assume innumerable forms according to thy desire. Thou Thyself art without beginning, and yet art the beginning of all. It is Thou who createth, preserveth, and destroyeth the world.

MAHĀNIRVĀṆA TANTRA

81 Invocation (*āvāhana*) or 'inviting' of the goddess Kālī. (Rice-paste drawing, Santhal house, Birbhum, West Bengal)

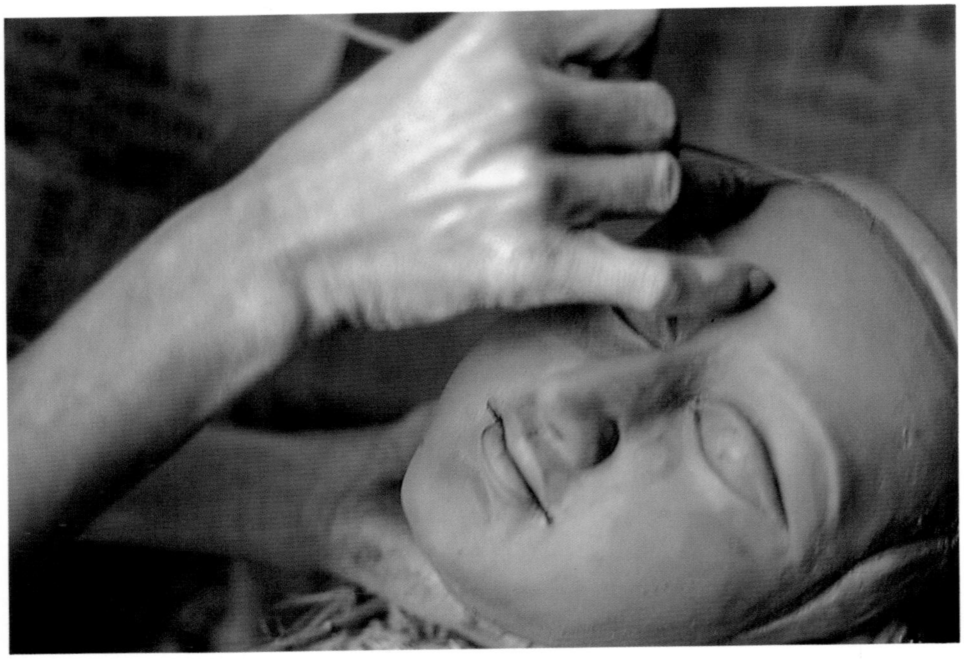

82 Putting the finishing touch on a devī-head. (Kumartuli, north Calcutta. Traditional form. Sun-baked clay)

83, 84 Workshop for the production of festival images. The daughter has been taught the traditional skills and will follow her father in taking charge of the family's production. (Kumartuli, north Calcutta)

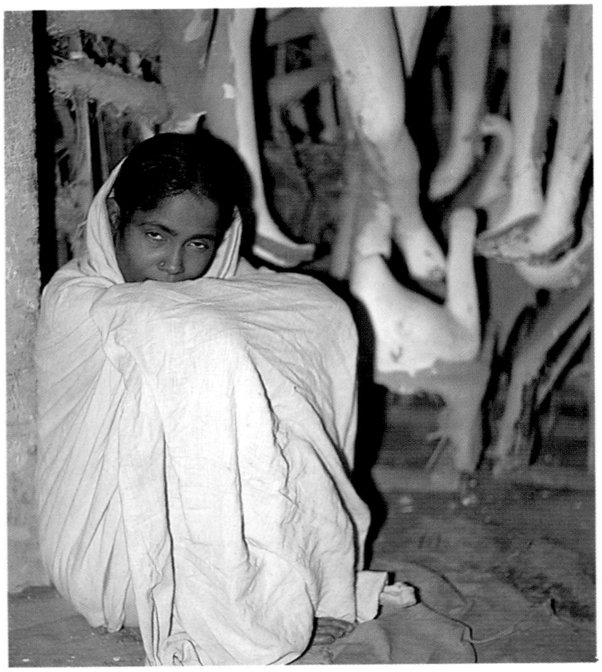

85 Face of a devī. (Kumartuli, north Calcutta. Traditional form. Painted sun-baked clay)

86 The gods beseech the daughter of the Himalayas to come to their aid against demonic power

87 The goddess in dialogue with herself

88 Durgā manifests herself, and is armed by all the gods

The story is told of how the great goddess Durgā, and Kālī the totality of all śaktis, the all-pervading energies that govern the universe, manifest themselves to rescue gods and men, who are helpless against demonic power.
Durgā is invoked by the gods, is armed for battle, and vanquishes the anti-gods with Kālī at her side

89 Durgā on her tiger-mount confronts her demon adversary

90 The goddess Durgā and Kālī in battle array

91 Durgā overpowers the Buffalo Demon

92 Kālī and Durgā triumphant in battle with the *asuras*

93, 94 Total self-surrender to the victorious goddess by gods and men

95 Visarjana. The departure of Durgā, her task completed

(Kangra, *c.* 18th century. Gouache on paper)

Visarjana, the rite of dissolution, the third and closing phase of all ritual worship

96 The Daśa-Mahāvidyās, 'Ten Great Wisdoms', each represented as a goddess. The first Mahāvidyā is Kālī. (Rajasthan, *c.* 19th century. Gouache on paper)

Each of the different goddesses holds the key to the transpersonal experience of the seeker

97 The fifth Mahāvidyā, Chinnamastā. (Kangra, *c.* 18th century. Gouache on paper)

The goddess Kālī – she without whom even the great god Śiva is as a corpse

'I prayed to Her, taking a flower in my hands: "Mother, here is Thy knowledge and here is Thy ignorance. Take them both, and give me only pure love. Here is Thy holiness and here is Thy unholiness. Take them both, Mother, and give me pure love. Here is Thy righteousness and here is Thy unrighteousness. Take them both, Mother, and give me pure love." I spoke of all these, but I could not say: "Mother, here is Thy truth and here is Thy falsehood, take them both." I gave up everything at Her feet but could not bring myself to give up truth.' (Prayer of Ramakrishna)

98, 99 The nineteenth-century mystic saint Ramakrishna, in trance-state before the icon of Kālī (opposite), at the Dakshineswar Temple of Kālī, north Calcutta

The festival of Durgā-pūjā. During the Navaratri (nine nights) of the popular festival, young girls receive the ritual worship of their families, as representing the goddess's maiden aspect. Thrown into water at the close of the worship, the images of Durgā are symbolically returned to the primordial source

100 The rite of Kumārī-pūjā, virgin worship. (Kangra, *c.* 18th century. Gouache on paper)

101 Festival image of Durgā being carried through the streets for the rite of immersion, visarjana, at the close of the Durgā-pūjā

102 Durgā-image inscribed with mantras chanted on sacred occasions and especially during the festival of Durgā-pūjā. (Rajasthan, *c.* 18th century. Gouache on cloth)

103 Lotus-emblem of the goddess. (Kangra, *c.* 18th century. Gouache on paper)

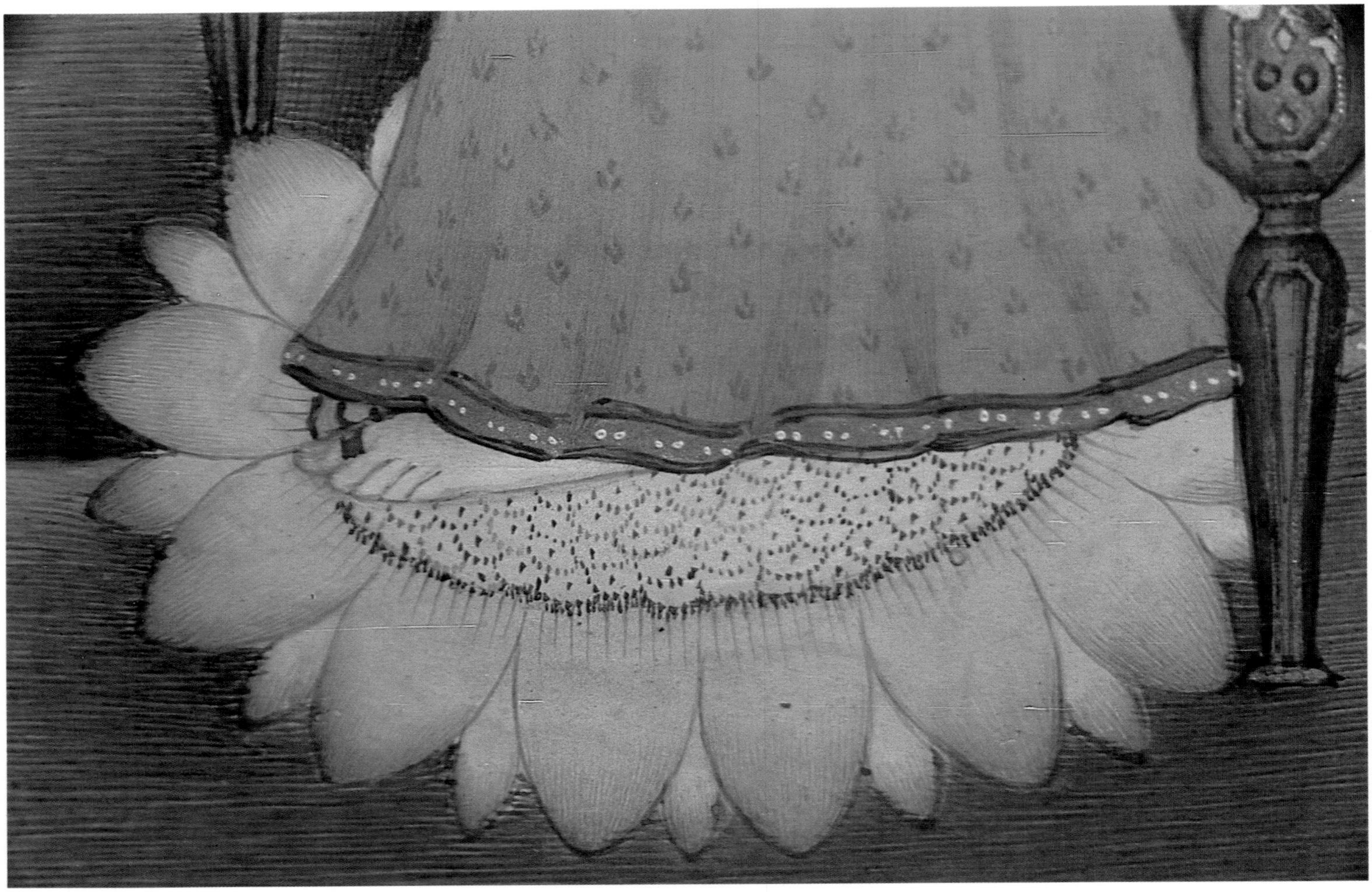

Plate 81
Offerings of flowers on a rice-paste drawing of a footprint invoke the Mother, the goddess Kālī, during her festival in October-November (Āswin-Kārtik). Invocation is essential, as the Mother is coming for a short period for the benefit of devotees.

Plates 82–85
Festival images of the goddesses are often modelled by hand, when no exact replicas are possible; others are replicated many times. Sometimes the head is cast from a mould, as here, while the lower portion is hand modelled. The variety and number of moulds are astonishing: it is in these that regional variations in the iconography are most marked.

The mould-patterns are traditional, handed down within a family over generations. Each family member, young or old, performs duties according to his or her capacity. This kind of communal effort is characteristic of traditional and folk art. The process of making the icons is not separate from worship. The preparation of the materials and all the stages of the manufacture are accompanied by rituals in order to imbue them with life-force. Between the raw material and the finished object lies a whole world of synthesis.

Plates 86–95
The account of the manifestation of the goddess Durgā (*Mārkaṇḍeya Purāṇa*) is chanted one hundred times during the main five days of the goddess's annual festival. The text is known as *Chaṇḍipātha* – 'Hymns to the Devi' – and is one of three main scriptures glorifying the goddess. The story of Durgā is told by the sage Medhasa to a king and a merchant who have taken refuge in his forest retreat. The account is organized into the classical form of a meditation on the three major aspects of the goddess: as Mahākālī, Mahālakshmī and Mahāsarasvatī.

The gods go to the Himalayas to pray to the daughter of the mountains for rescue from the demons' tyranny. There Śiva and all the gods send forth their powers in the form of streams of flames, combining themselves into a mass of smoke which grows until it condenses into the shape of the goddess Durgā. Her many arms hold auspicious weapons and emblems, jewels and ornaments, garments and utensils, garlands and rosaries of beads, all offered by the gods. In the terrific battle with the demons that follows, Durgā destroys the dark forces to rescue gods and men. In this context, the goddess Kālī, born from her brow, is considered the Terrible form of the Great Goddess Durgā. Her task fulfilled, Durgā immerses herself in the waters and departs (*visarjana*). The place of her disappearance is marked with an open lotus. Every occasion of ritual worship begins with invocation of the deity, and ends with the rite of visarjana.

Plates 96–97
Specific *Tantras* are devoted to each of the Ten Mahāvidyās, explaining their natures, yantras, modes of ritual and the benefits that are to be gained from their worship. The first Mahāvidyā is Kālī herself. The fifth Mahāvidyā is Chinnamastā, who symbolizes the end of one existence and the beginning of the next. The opposites Rati and Kāma, the feminine and masculine principles, lying conjoined beneath her feet, represent the transcending of all polarities, and female ascendancy for the sake of creation.

Plate 98
Ramakrishna, the great nineteenth-century mystic (1836-1886), served in his youth as a temple-priest in the Kālī Temple at Dakshineswar, north of Calcutta. He would meditate for long hours before the image of the goddess Kālī (plate 99), and came to look upon her as his mother and the mother of the universe. He saw that the image lived and breathed, heard and understood him. He would sing hymns, talk and pray to her till he lost all consciousness of the outer world. Often he would cry in his fervent desire to be vouchsafed a vision of the goddess. One day while in a trance he was rewarded for his devotion. The

Mother Kālī revealed herself to him face to face, a 'limitless, infinite, effulgent ocean of spirit'. From then on, the sight of her image or the mere mention of her name was enough to throw him into a trance. He began to neglect his formal temple duties and so lost his position. For twelve years he devoted himself to meditation and tantric ritual practices in a nearby wood (Pañchavati, or 'Five Trees'). Of this period he said that 'it was as if a great spiritual tornedo raged within'. He practised the teachings of many divergent sects within Hinduism, and through each of them achieved the same supreme realization. He sought to induce a vision of Muhammad. With this in view he underwent religious discipline under a Muslim saint, and 'accepted' Islam. In like manner he experienced Christianity, read the Bible with a friend, meditated on a picture of the Madonna and Child, and was vouchsafed a vision of Jesus, during which a voice said to him: 'This is the Christ who poured out his heart's blood for the redemption of mankind.' He arrived at the conclusion that all religions contain the same truth. In Ramakrishna's words: 'As many faiths, so many paths', to reach one and the same goal. He saw god in everything, and would sometimes place flowers on his own head and worship himself, spending many hours in the trance-state. After Ramakrishna's death, his student-disciple Swami Vivekananda became internationally famous. He stressed the divine in every human being, and carried the teaching of Ramakrishna to all parts of the world.

Plate 99
Kālī, the Terrible form of the Great Goddess, appears as enchantress, mother and destroyer. She inspires awe and love. Though her image is filled with terrifying symbols, their real meaning is not as at first appears. They have equivocal significance. Kālī is the symbol of the cosmic power of time (Kāla), and in this aspect she signifies annihilation. Yet through death the seed of life emerges. Kālī is the embodiment of creation, preservation and annihilation. She is represented as black because, 'Just as all colours disappear in black, so all names and forms disappear in Her' (*Mahānirvāṇa Tantra*). In tantric rituals she is described as garbed in space (*digambari*). In her nakedness, she is free from all the veils of illusion. Her dishevelled hair (*elokeshī*) forms a curtain of death which surrounds life in mystery. Her garland of fifty human heads, each representing one of the fifty letters of the Sanskrit alphabet, symbolizes power and knowledge. The letters are nuclear sound-vibrations indicating the power of mantras. She wears a 'girdle of human hands'. Hands are the principal instruments of work, and so signify the action of karma or accumulated deeds, constantly reminding the viewer that ultimate freedom is conditioned by one's actions. Her three eyes govern the three forces of past, present and future. Her white teeth are symbolic of *sattva*, the transclucent intelligence-stuff, suppressing her tongue which is red, indicative of *rajas*, a determinate level of existence leading downwards to *tamas*, inertia. Kālī has four hands: a left hand holds a severed head, indicating annihilation of evil power; another left hand carries the sword of physical extermination, with which she cuts the thread of bondage. Her two right hands dispel fear and exhort to spiritual strength. She is the changeless, limitless primordial power (*ādyā-śakti*) awakening the unmanifested Śiva lying passive beneath her feet. In this image she symbolizes all-pervading, all-embracing power.

Plate 100
A naked girl adorned with jewels was worshipped by the Śākta sect as an incarnation of the Mother Goddess in her maiden aspect, and hence of cosmic energy. In the illustration the virgin for Kumārī-pūjā (virgin worship) is depicted between two birds, symbols of the liberated soul. This ancient rite is recalled during the annual festival of Durgā, when young girls dressed in new clothes receive the ritual worship of their families.

Plates 101–103
The goddess Durgā is worshipped with seven hundred mantras from the scriptures, especially during her nine-day festival. At the end of the Durgā-pūjā, images of the goddess are carried through the streets to be cast into the temple-tank or river. In the concluding ceremony, the image that was infused with life-force and became an emblem of cosmic realities is forsaken in the rite of *visarjana*. The dissolution of the image and its return to the primordial source from which it arose, symbolize the merging of one's own consciousness with the cosmic consciousness. The One for whom all the rituals and devotion were practised is now immersed in one's own inner self, as one bids farewell to outward worship.

Yantra of Durgā

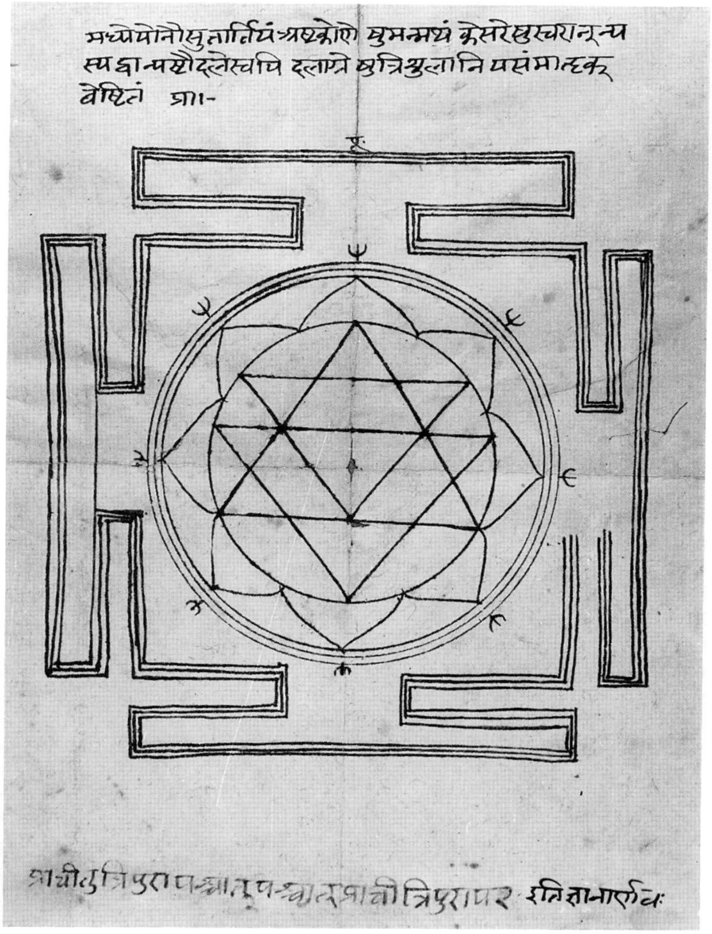

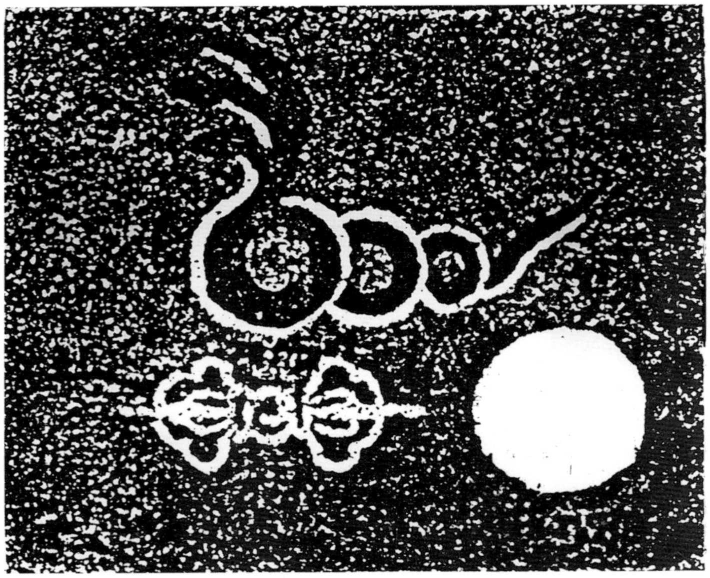

Chapter Eight

Syncretism

Hinduism is multidimensional. Its active elements include the heritage of the ancient Dravidian and Vedic cultures, Jainism and Buddhism, Esotericism and Tantrism, down to popular local cults. Indian schools of thought are the materials from which a way of life is constructed, and ritual observance is the living tradition by which it is maintained. Great stress is laid upon the performance of ritual, which is believed to unite people of different beliefs in a spiritual community.

During the course of history once-separate deities have become fused. The Vedic Dyāvāpṛithivī, for example, is a combination of Dyaus, Sky, and Pṛithivī, Earth; Indrāgni, a combination of Indra and Agni. In later times such fusions indicate the syncretism of different sects, as with Hari and Hara (Vishṇu and Śiva), Kālī-Kṛishṇa, Rāma-Kṛishṇa and Gaur-Hari (Chaitanya and Kṛishṇa). Some of the chief deities were grouped in triads, of which the best known is Trimūrti consisting of Brahmā (the Creator), Vishṇu (the Preserver), and Śiva (the Destroyer).

Popular Hinduism groups together even larger numbers of deities. The ritual known as *Pañchāyatana*, 'Five Bodies', requires the invocation of a sacred pentad represented by small images, or symbols drawn on the floor. The five deities are Gaṇeśa, who is usually invoked at the very commencement of the worship, Vishṇu, Śiva, Durgā and Sūrya. One of the deities will be regarded as the special patron of the devotee, and a symbol of that deity is placed in the centre.

India's powerful deities are often represented in animal form, and it is held that all life is interrelated, since all life is an expression of the Ultimate Reality. Worship creates a relationship with all life, and even with inanimate objects.

A devotee will have his or her own 'chosen deity' (*ishṭa-devatā*), yet will always pay equal homage to other deities. In this manner, Hinduism remains a vital syncretic force.

Unified am I, quite undivided,
unified my soul,
unified my sight, unified my hearing,
unified my breathing – both in and out,
unified is my continuous breath.
Unified, quite undivided am I,
the whole of me.

ATHARVA VEDA

The conception of masculinity and femininity as two divisible qualities is as illusory as the idea of the duality of body and soul, matter and energy. The hermaphroditic image of Śiva and Pārvatī signifies psychic totality

PREVIOUS PAGE

104 Ardhanārīśvara: the god Śiva and goddess Pārvatī as hermaphrodite. (Chola, 11-12th century. Bronze)

105 Harihara, representing the bi-unity of Śiva and Vishṇu. (Basohli school, Jammu-Kashmir, *c.* 18th century. Gouache on paper)

106 Garuḍa, mythical bird and vehicle of Vishṇu. (Kangra school, *c.* 18th century. Gouache on paper)

The triple head of the elephant-god, the monkey-god and the boar (Vishṇu-avatar) stands for the syncretism of three cults, but equally, for a cultural synthesis. 'Three Forms' synthesizes the three cosmic phases of creation, preservation and dissolution

107 Gaṇeśa the elephant-god combined with Hanumān the monkey-god and the boar incarnation of Vishṇu. (Nepal, *c.* 17th century. Bronze)

108 Trimūrti, 'Three-Forms', a tribal bronze reminiscent of the three-faced Maheśa of the Śiva Temple of the Elephanta Cave, near Bombay. (Bastar, Madhya Pradesh, *c.* 19th century)

The heads of the Supreme Śiva, the colossal figure of the Jain saint of the highest order, and the image of the Buddha in the posture of contemplation (plate 111), suggest in their ineffable serenity a vision of unity, and of one divinized humanity

109 Heads of Sadāśiva, combining Śiva as Mahādeva with Bhairava and the Great Goddess Umā. (Kashmir, *c.* 8th century. Stone)

110 Gomaṭeśvara, a Jain saint worshipped daily by pilgrims. (Sravanabelgola, Karnataka, *c.* AD. 983. Stone)

111 The Buddha in the posture of contemplation. (Gandhara school. *c.* 400. Stone)

Plate 104
God and goddess, Śiva and Pārvatī, jointly worshipped are represented as the half-male, half-female deity Ardhanārīśvara.

Plate 105
Harihara represents the bi-unity of Vishṇu (Hari) and Śiva (Hara). Merged in the ritual of Pañchāyatana, they symbolize the eternal cycle of preservation and dissolution, of birth and rebirth.

Plate 106
The mythical bird Garuḍa is half giant, half eagle, and carries within his body gods and goddesses, positive and negative forces, so representing a world of synthesis and the abolition of sectarian rivalries.

Plate 107
The triple-headed figure indicates a synthesis of the three cults of Gaṇapati (Gaṇeśa), Hanumān (the monkey-hero of the *Rāmāyaṇa*) and Varāha (the third, boar incarnation of Vishṇu). *Gaṇa* means 'category', and Gaṇapati is the lord of the category of comprehension, through which the relation between the microcosm and the macrocosm is comprehended. For the Gāṇapatya sect he is the Supreme. In any rite, Gaṇeśa is regarded as one of the chief five deities. Gaṇeśa or Gaṇapati has two energy-consorts: Success (Siddhī), and Prosperity (Ṛiddhi). He always overcomes obstacles, and so is invoked at the commencement of any ritual or enterprise. To this day, in all sacramental prayers the first invocation is for the elephant-headed, serpent-garlanded and four-armed red and white deity Gaṇeśa, a popular god who knows no caste-distinction. One Gāṇapatya sect combines the worship of Śakti and Gaṇapati.

Plate 108–109
Trimūrti (Three Forms), whether a tribal deity or mighty Śiva, is a synthesis of three deities representing three aspects of reality. The eighth-century heads of Sadāśiva combine Śiva as Mahādeva, centre, with Bhairava on the right and the Great Goddess Umā on the left.

Plate 110
Ṛishabha, or Ādinātha, 'first lord', Jain saint of the present cosmic cycle, renounced his kingdom in favour of his eldest son Bharata to live the life of an ascetic. Bharata's brother Gomaṭeśvara is also a renowned Jain saint. His colossal statue, the tallest monolithic carving in the world, stands fifty-seven feet high. It shows the saint in the *sthāna*, or stance, of *kāyotsarga*, 'body-liberation'. He stands upright with feet firmly planted, arms at his sides but not touching his body. He is space-clad, and in profound meditation. Creepers entwine themselves around his legs and arms, while he remains undisturbed and serene, comprehending all things, unlimited by time, space and object. A temple built at the feet of the image maintains uninterrupted ritual worship of the saint. Every fifteen years the saint's head is ritually showered with milk mixed with clarified butter, sweet spices and silver coins, by thousands of pilgrims who mount a specially erected scaffolding to make their offerings.

Plate 111
Buddhism, like Jainism, is a living force side by side with Hinduism. At the age of twenty-nine Siddhārtha Gautama, who was to become Buddha, 'went out from home to homelessness'. At the age of thirty-five he attained Bodhi (Enlightenment) or Saṁbodhi (Full Enlightenment). Near the banks of the Niranjana River in Bodhgaya he sat down to meditate under the shade-giving fig tree, and resolved to remain there until Enlightenment came to him. This tree later became known as the Bo or Bodhi tree, because it was under its branches that, after seven weeks of profound meditation, he at last obtained the supreme knowledge he sought. From then on he was honoured as the Buddha (Enlightened One). This Buddha image is in dhyāna-mudrā, contemplative posture.

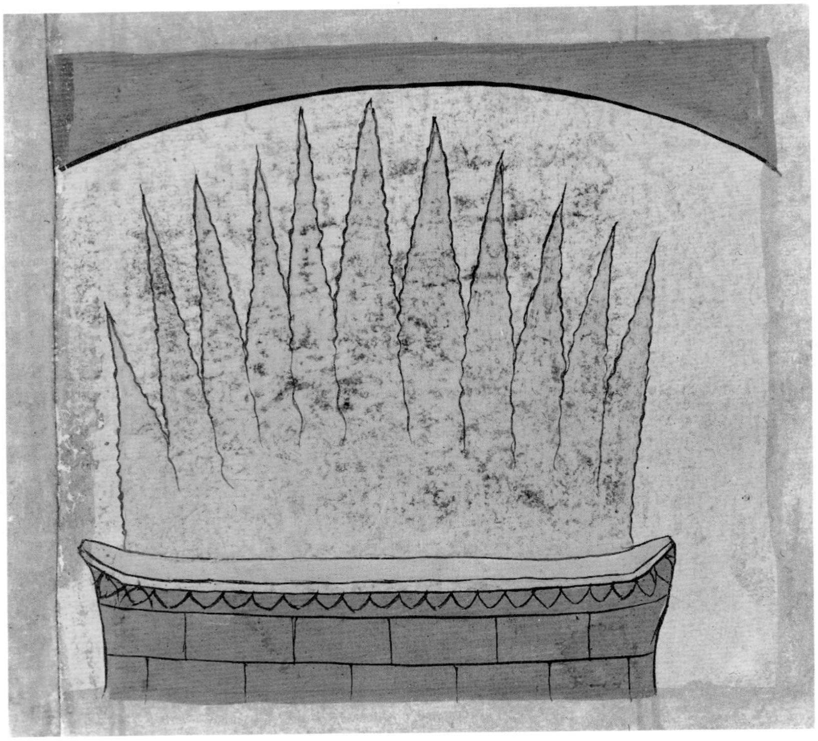

Chapter Nine

Death and Rebirth

From conception to cremation, the whole span of human life is marked by appropriate rites. There is scarcely any aspect of existence which has not been so regulated. Elaborate rites are connected with the pre-natal state, with birth, growth, adolescence, marriage and household life, with retreats, renunciations and finally, with death. Domestic rites are performed at each stage of development, until at last the body is dissolved back into the elements of which it is composed. Death is not the end of an individual, but a new start in a dynamic process. According to the *Bhagavadgītā*, it is a change of old clothes for new.

Biologically, every moment of life is also a death. Death brings new life to birth. That is why the funeral rite, *antyeshṭi*, is a rite of passage. The individual, like every aspect of the world, comes into being, develops, disappears and is reborn. The course of the next life is determined by the present one. Until liberation is achieved, the sum total of karmic action in the present life influences the pattern of future existence.

Death is therefore only a 'way-station'. In the *Kaṭha Upanishad* the young Nachiketas questions Yama, the King of the Dead, and is told that the Ātman, the true self and a spark of Brahman, the Universal Self, never dies at the death of the body. It is timeless and unending. The rituals of death point to life's unity, with a vision of eternal reality, Brahman.

The soul is not born, nor does it die. That self has not come from anywhere, has not become anyone. Unborn, changeless, primeval, everlasting, that self is not slain when the body is slain.

KAṬHA UPANISHAD

'When the heart weeps for what it has lost, the spirit laughs for what it has found.' – Sufi aphorism

112 Maṇikarṇikā Burning Ghāṭ,
Banaras

113 Offerings for the ancestors set afloat on the Ganges River at Hardwar

114 Ritual offerings on human skulls, placed under the banyan tree at Aghori Ashram, Bakreswar Temple, West Bengal

115 Tableau symbolizing birth, death, and rebirth. (Bakreswar Temple, West Bengal)

116 Sāvitrī with her husband, whom she regains from Yama, God of Death. (Bakreswar Temple, West Bengal. Contemporary expression of traditional form. Painted clay)

Rites of passage. Individual and universe obey the same laws and follow the same pattern. Here lies eternal flux, transformation, the rhythms of coming and going. The sum total of karmic action in the present life influences the pattern of existence of the next one. But if an individual receives the supreme realization, he or she 'will not return'. The state of 'no return' depends on individual progress in liberation techniques, of which a major one is ritual. The greater the intensity of the ritual experience, the higher will be the spiritual growth, until the cycle of birth and rebirth comes to an end. Ritual has the power to vanquish the fear of death, and to transcend death, in the experience of life's unity

117 The voyage of the souls of the ancestors, and the performance of *antyeshṭi* ceremonies to assist them on their journey. (Nepal, *c.* 18th century. Gouache on paper)

118 A tower near the Harishchandra Burning Ghāṭ in which rites are performed to give peace to the departed souls. (Banaras)

119 Memorial posts. (Kumartuli, north Calcutta. Contemporary expression of traditional form. Carved and painted wood)

Notes on plates 112–119

Plate 112
The sights and sounds of the cremation ground stress the truth of bodily transience. Yet fear, revulsion and grief can be the conditions for an explosion of psychic potential, and for reconciliation and renewal.

Plate 113
At pilgrimage-places such as Hardwar, Mathura or Banaras, lighted lamps with flowers are set afloat on the river current, while the name of the deceased is held up in a rite of homage to the ancestors.

Plate 114
Rows of human skulls under the banyan tree receive ritual offerings from passers-by. They help to obliterate distinctions between the objects of attraction and revulsion, and suggest that all ostensibly positive and negative aspects of existence form an inseparable whole.

Plate 115
The tableau of birth, represented by holes, death symbolized by a sacrificial altar, and rebirth suggested by a laid-out bed, gives the sense of passage and of human participation in the cosmic order.

Plate 116
The story of Sāvitrī, daughter of a king of Madra, is told in the *Mahābhārata*. She fell in love and married, but had been warned by a sage that her husband Satyavān was not fated to live beyond a day a few months hence. She awaited the time with penances and fasting, and when the appointed day dawned, refused to leave her husband's side, going with him to the forest to gather food and fuel. In the midst of his labours the husband fell down in a faint. Sāvitrī took him in her arms and sat under a banyan tree to await the coming of Yama, God of Death. When the god carried off the soul of Satyavān, Sāvitrī followed him. Yama offered her gifts: sight for her blind father-in-law and the restoration of his lost kingdom, and for herself, a hundred sons. She accepted all the gifts, saying: 'You have promised me sons, and this promise cannot be fulfilled unless my husband is restored to me.' Yama relented, and Satyavān was permitted to return to the world of the living.

The theme of death and return to life occurs with variants in the myths of many times and places. It provides the framework for sacred mysteries in which neophytes experience symbolic death and rebirth as a discipline for spiritual development.

Plate 117
Pilgrims seeking release from the cycle of birth and rebirth undertake pilgrimages to rivers, temple-tanks or lakes. A popular belief is that by immersion in the sacred waters one may gain liberation irrespective of one's previous good or bad deeds, one's karmic action. Those who attain a higher plane may 'cross the river' to reach Indraloka or Devaloka, and those who voyage in the ship of knowledge and understanding will not return. A pilgrimage-centre is known as *tīrtha*, meaning a bathing place or ford.

Plate 118
The last rites to speed the departing soul, *antyeshṭi*, are performed by the priest in towers at the burning ghāṭ.

Plate 119
Painted wooden mortuary posts are placed at the junction of three or four roads, or in cremation grounds, particularly in rural Bengal and Assam. Usually a male or female figure is carved at the base, a bull at the centre, a Śiva-liṅga or an image of Śiva-Pārvatī at the top, ending with a pyramid or pointed finial.

Chapter Ten

Bliss-consciousness

According to the Indian conception, the cosmos is to be viewed as a continuum. Like a circle or ovoid, the universal order presents an uninterrupted continuity. While there are three phases of the cosmic process – emanation, preservation and reabsorption – no phase is absolute in itself, but each contains all the parts of the whole. In the microcosm of ritual worship, each of the three phases – of invoking, entertaining and dismissing the deity – contains the whole of which it is a part. The significance of ritual at all levels is holistic.

Nor is there a break anywhere in the chain of existential forms; and, above all, each link in that chain is formed in the image of each of its parts. An individual is a universe in miniature, a complete and divine image of the entire cosmos.

All Indian ritual practices are linked to the vision of a rhythmical, cyclical order – the *līlā* or 'play' of the universe. The chief goal of ritual worship is to experience this order, to feel the interrelation of all phenomena, to make the transition from an egocentric to a cosmocentric outlook – to merge self in the whole. Through a dynamic process of awakening and self-liberation, one may ultimately discover one's true identity, which is a state of *ānanda* – transcendent bliss or joy.

Ānanda is not absolutely different from or unconnected with the joy that we experience in ordinary consciousness, the joy which makes life worth living. Reality is *satcitānanda* – *sat*, being; *cit*, consciousness; and *ānanda*, bliss. The measure of Bliss-consciousness is the measure of one's spiritual development. Ritual and its aesthetic reinforce, purify and expand Bliss-consciousness, without limit. Only when joy becomes unconditional and pure, and constitutes the entire nature of the self, is self returned to its primal oneness with the All.

From joy springs all creation,
by joy it is sustained,
towards joy it proceeds,
and to joy it returns.

Muṇḍaka Upanishad

PREVIOUS PAGE
120 Spiral galaxy

Through ritual we may share in the quintessential, rhythmical līlā (play) of the universe, and experience ecstasy. We are told of Ramakrishna getting down from his carriage on occasion to dance with drunkards in the street – their reeling joy, so different in source and qualities, transporting him to a state of divine bliss

121 Kṛishṇa, the embodiment of divinity and love, at the centre of the maṇḍala, dancing with Rādhā, *hlādinī-śakti*, the Beauty of the World. (Jaipur, *c.* 1840. Gouache on paper)

122 Śiva as Natarāja, Lord of Dance. (South India, 10th century. Bronze)

123 Yab-yum. (Nepal, *c.* 17th century. Wood)

124 Mithuna (loving couple), expressing the abolition of the experience of duality. (Sun Temple, Konarak, Orissa, 13th century. Stone)

OVERLEAF
125 Pure consciousness, the metacosmic void. (Rajasthan, *c.* 18th century. Gouache on paper)

126 Śakti. (West Bengal, *c.* 5th century. Terracotta)

It is by losing the egocentric life that we save the hitherto latent and undiscovered life which, in the spiritual part of our being, we share with the divine Ground. This new-found life is more abundant than the other, and of a different and higher kind. Its possession is liberation into the eternal, and liberation is beatitude. Necessarily so; for the Brahman, who is one with the Ātman, is not only Being and knowledge, but also Bliss.

ALDOUS HUXLEY

127 Sannyāsi performing ritual oblation beside the Ganges River at Hrisikesh

Notes on plates 120–127

Plate 120
In the galaxy as within the atom, all is in constant motion, all is interconnected.

Plate 121
Kṛishṇa dancing with Rādhā miraculously multiplies himself for the circle of waiting gopīs (milkmaids), revealing himself to each by his power of māyā (illusion). As primal cosmic joy, the Supreme Kṛishṇahood is the point of consciousness in which the male and female principles (Kṛishṇa-Rādhā) unite. Under the spell of creative play (*līlā*) of the Supreme, the outward-directed world of multiplicity and separatedness returns toward the inward focus of unity, towards the ultimate centre, the centre of selfless 'love'. It is believed that the universe has come into existence by the pouring out of joy, is sustained by joy and will be reabsorbed into joy.

Plates 122
Energy is matter, matter energy. Śiva as Natarāja, Lord of Dance, executes the cosmic dance that typifies the rhythmic movement of the universe. The circle springing from the lotus base, symbol of manifestation, is ringed with flames – symbol of cosmic energies. In his upper right hand Śiva holds the drum, representing vibration in space (*ākāśa*), the first of the five elements which announces creation, and in the palm of his upper left hand, he shows a flame – symbol of the final conflagration of this present created world. His lower right hand is raised in *avaya mudrā*, the gesture giving freedom from fear, while his lower left arm, crossing the body, points to the left foot held aloft, a symbol of release. His right foot is firmly planted on a dwarf, the demon of forgetfulness. The cosmos is his theatre: dancing, he sustains its manifold phenomena. Creating, manifesting, veiling, unveiling and destroying, he dances the world into and out of existence. Dancing, he veils ultimate reality and unveils it for his devotees, who recognize in the heart-maddening dancing the dance of bliss (*ānanda-tāṇḍava*).

Plates 123–124
The union of masculine and feminine principles, expressing the return to wholeness, is reflected on the human level as the loving couple (*mithuna*). In tantric ritual every conjunction of opposites is a joyful transcending of the phenomenal world.

Plates 125–126
Wholeness-without-qualities is experienced as *ānanda*, or Bliss-consciousness: 'The ego has disappeared, I have realized my identity and so all my desires have melted away. I have risen above my ignorance and my knowledge of this seeming universe. What is this joy I feel? Who shall measure it? I know nothing but joy, limitless, unbounded I.' – Śaṅkara (*c.* AD 686).

Plate 127
At the foot of the Himalayas a *sannyāsi* or renunciate performs his daily ritual, offering flowers to the River Ganges whose water fills the copper ritual vessel. He has renounced all possessions, even his name. He lives on fruits or milk, and the plants he gathers, and sleeps on the ground. Never angry or perturbed, he exists in peace and mental tranquility, to merge at last with the changeless, the All.

BIBLIOGRAPHY

GLOSSARY

INDEX

BIBLIOGRAPHY

Agrawala, Vasudeva S., *Sparks From the Vedic Fire*, Varanasi 1962.

Aiyangar, Narayana, *Essays on Indo-Aryan Mythology*, Vol. II, Madras 1901.

Aiyangar, T. R. Srinivasa, trans., *Śaiva Upaniṣads*, Madras 1953.

——, *Vaiṣṇava Upaniṣads*, Madras 1945.

——, *Yoga Upaniṣads*, Madras 1952.

Aiyar, P. S. Sivasvami, *Evolution of Hindu Moral Ideals*, Calcutta 1935.

Apte, V. M., *Social and Religious Life in the Gṛhya-Sūtras*, Bombay 1954.

Auboyer, Jeannine, *Daily Life in Ancient India* (trans. S. W. Taylor), London 1965.

Aurobindo, Sri, *The Problem of Rebirth*, Pondicherry 1952.

Ayyar, Narayana, *The Origin and Early History of Saivism in South India*, Madras 1936.

Ayyar, P. V. Jagadisa, *South Indian Festivals*, Madras 1931.

Bagchi, Prabodh Chandra, trans., *Pre-Aryan and Pre-Dravidian in India*, Calcutta 1929.

Banerjee, Jitendranath, *The Development of Hindu Iconography*, Calcutta 1956.

——, *Paurānic and Tantric Religion (Early Phase)*, Calcutta 1966.

Basham, A. L., *The Wonder that was India*, London 1954.

Bhattacharyya, Bhabatosh, *Studies in Dharmaśāstra*, Calcutta 1964.

Bhattacharyya, H.D., 'Minor Religious Sects' in *The History and Culture of the Indian People*. Vol. III, Bombay 1954.

Bhattacharyya, Kokileswar, *An Introduction to Advaita Philosophy*, Calcutta 1924.

Bhattacharyya, N. N., *History of the Tantric Religion*, New Delhi 1982.

Bhattacharyya, P., *Ideals of Indian Womanhood*, Calcutta 1921.

Bhattacharyya, Vidhushekara, *The Basic Conception of Buddhism*, Calcutta 1934.

Bhandarkar, Ramakrishna Gopal, *Vaisnavism, Saivism and Minor Religious Systems*, Strasbourg 1913.

Brahma, Nalini Kanta, *The Philosophy of Hindu Sadhana*, London 1932.

Brockington, J. L., *The Sacred Thread (Hinduism in its Continuity and Diversity)*, Edinburgh 1981.

Brown, W. Norman, *Man in the Universe: Some Cultural Continuities in India*, Berkeley 1966.

Cambell, Joseph, *The Masks of God: Oriental Mythology*, New York and London 1962.

Capra, Fritjof, *The Turning Point*, New York and London 1982.

Chakravarti, Chintaharan, 'Ideals of Tantra Rites', *The Indian Historical Quarterly*, Vol. 10, pp. 486–92.

Chatterji, Suniti Kumar, *The Indian Synthesis, and Racial and Cultural Intermixture in India*, Ahmedabad 1939.

Clothey, Fred W., *The Many Faces of Murukan: The History and Meaning of a South Indian God*, The Hague 1978.

Coomaraswamy, Ananda K., *The Dance of Shiva*, New Delhi, 1976.

——, 'The Tantric Doctrines of Divine Biunity', *Annals of the Bhandarkar Oriental Research Institute*, Vol. 19, 1938, pp. 173–83.

——, *Time and Eternity*, Ascona, Switzerland 1947.

——, *The Transformation of Nature in Art*, Cambridge, Mass., 1934.

Crooke, William, *An Introduction to the Popular Religion and Folk-Lore of Northern India*, Westminster 1896.

Daniélou, Alain, *Hindu Polytheism*, London 1964.

Das, Sudhendukumar, *Śakti or Divine Power*, Calcutta 1934.

Dasgupta, Shashi Bhushan, *Obscure Religious Cults*, Calcutta 1962.

Dasgupta, Surendra Nath, *Hindu Mysticism*, Chicago 1927.

——, and S. K. De, *Indian Idealism*, Cambridge 1933.

Datta, Bhupendra Nath, *Dialectics of Hindu Rituals*, Calcutta 1950.

Dazian, S. G., *The Ganges in Myth and History*, Honolulu 1978.

Devanandan, P. D., *The Concept of Māyā*, London 1950.

Deutsch, Eliot S., 'Śakti in Medieval Hindu Sculpture' in *The Journal of Aesthetics and Art Criticism*, Fall 1965, pp. 81–9.

Devi, Akshaya-Kumari, *The Evolution of the Rigvedic Pantheon*, Calcutta 1938.

Diehl, C. G., 'The Goddess of Forests in Tamil Literature' in *Tamil Culture*, XI (1964), pp. 308–16.

——, *Instrument and Purpose: Studies on Rites and Rituals in South India*, Lund 1956.

Dimmitt, Cornelia, and J. A. B. van Buitenen, eds. *Classical Hindu Mythology*, Philadelphia 1978.

Dimock, E. C., *The Place of the Hidden Moon: Erotic Mysticism in the Vaiṣṇava-Sahajiya Cult of Bengal*, Chicago 1966.

Drury, Naama, *The Sacrificial Ritual in the Śatapatha Brāhmaṇa*, Delhi 1981.

Dumont, L., 'World Renunciation in Indian Religions' in *Contributions to Indian Sociology*, No. 4, 1960.

Eaton, Gai, *The Richest Vein, Eastern Tradition and Modern Thought*, London 1949.

Ehrenfels, O. R., *Mother-right in India*, Hyderabad 1941.
Eliade, Mircea, *The Sacred and the Profane*, New York 1961.
——, *Myth of the Eternal Return*, tr. Willard R. Trask, Princeton and London 1955.
Elmore, Wilburn Theodore, *Dravidian Gods in Modern Hinduism*, Madras 1925.
Embree, Ainslie T., ed., *The Hindu Tradition*, New York 1966.
Faddegon, B., *The Vaiçesika System*, Amsterdam 1918.
Fergusson, James, *Tree and Serpent Worship*, London 1873.
Gandhi, Indira, and Jean-Louis Nou, *Inde: Hommes, Rites et Dieux*, Vilo 1978.
Getty, Alice, *Ganeśa: A Monograph on the Elephant-faced God*, Oxford 1936.
Ghosha, Pratapchandra, *Durgā Pūjā*, Calcutta 1841.
Glasenapp, Helmuth von, *Brahma and Buddha*, Berlin 1926.
Gonda, J., *Change and Continuity in Indian Religion*, The Hague 1965.
——, *Vedic Ritual*, Leiden, 1980.
Griffith, R. T. H., trans., *The Rāmāyana of Vālmiki*, 5 vols., London 1870–4.
Guenon, René, *Introduction to the Study of the Hindu Doctrines*, trans. Marco Pallis, London 1945.
Gupta, Shakti M., *Plant Myths and Traditions in India*, London 1971.
Gupte, B. A., *Hindu Holidays and Ceremonials*, Calcutta 1916.
Hardy, Frianhelm, *Viraha-Bhakti (The Early History of Kṛṣṇa Devotion in South India)*, Delhi 1983.
Harrison, Max Hunter, *Indian Monism and Pluralism*, London 1932.
Heiman, Betty, *Indian and Western Philosophy, a study in contrasts*, London 1937.
Humphreys, Christmas, *Karma and Rebirth*, London 1959.
Huntington, R., 'Avatāras and Yugas: Purāṇic Cosmology', *Purāṇa* 6, 1964, pp. 7–39.
In the Image of Man: *The Indian Perception of the Universe Through 2,000 Years of Painting and Sculpture*. Festival of India Catalogue published by Arts Council of Great Britain in association with Weidenfeld and Nicolson, London 1982.
Jackson, R. J., *India's Quest for Reality*, London 1938.
Jash, J. S., *Reincarnation and Karma*, New York 1956.
Jayakar, Pupul, *The Earthen Drum*, New Delhi 1982.
Jha, Ganganatha, *Shaṅkara Vedanta*, Allahabad 1939.
Jones, John Peter, *India: Its Life and Thought*, New York 1908.
Jung, C. G., *Modern Man in Search of a Soul*, London 1933.
Kabir, Humayun, *The Indian Heritage*, Bombay 1955.
Kamasūtra of Vātsyāyana, ed. P. Durgaparada, Bombay 1891.
Kamath, M. A., *Hinduism and Modern Science*, Mangalore 1947.
Kaviraj, Dr Gopi Nath, *Puja-Tattva (Essence of Worship)*, Varanasi 1976.
Khanna, Madhu, *Yantra*, London and New York 1979.
Kosambi, Damodar Dharmanand, *An Introduction to the Study of Indian History*, Bombay 1956.
——, *Myth and Reality*, Bombay 1962.
Kramrisch, Stella, *The Presence of Śiva*, Princeton 1981.
Krishna Shastri, H., *South Indian Images of Gods and Goddesses*, Madras 1916.
Lal, Shyam Kishore, *Female Divinities in Hindu Mythology and Ritual*, Pune 1980.
Maitra, Harendranath, *Hinduism: The World Ideal*, London 1916.
Maitra, Susil Kumar, *Fundamental Questions of Indian Metaphysics and Logic*, Calcutta 1956.
Maity, Pradyot Kumar, *Historical Studies in the Cult of the Goddess Manasā*, Calcutta 1966.
Marshall, Sir John, *Mohenjo-Daro and the Indus Civilization*, 3 vols. London 1931.
Matilal, B. K., *Nyāya-Vaiśeṣika*, Wiesbaden 1977.
Maxwell, T. S., 'Transformation Aspects of Hindu Myth and Iconology: Viśvarūpa' in *Art and Archaeology Research Papers*, 4 (December 1973), pp. 59–79.
Meyer, Johann Jacob, *Sexual Life in Ancient India: A Study in the Comparative History of Indian Culture*, London 1930.
Mishra, Umesha, *Conception of Matter According to Nyaya-Vaicesika*, Allahabad 1936.
Mohan, Simha, *The Mysticism of Time in Rig Veda*, Lahore 1939.
Monier-Williams, Sir Monier, *Hinduism*, Calcutta 1877.
——, *Religious Thought and Life in India, I, Vedism, Brahmanism and Hinduism*, London 1885.
Mookerjee, Ajit, *Folk Art of Bengal* (New and revised), Calcutta 1946.
——, *Indian Primitive Art*, Calcutta 1959.
——, *Kundalini*, London and New York 1983.
——, and Madhu Khanna, *The Tantric Way*, London and New York 1977.
Müller, Friedrich Max, *The Six Systems of Indian Philosophy*, London 1928.
Nehru, Jawaharlal, *The Unity of India*, London 1941.
Neumann, E., *The Great Mother*, New York 1961.
Nikhilananda, Swami, *The Essence of Hinduism*, New York 1946.
——, trans., *The Gospel of Ramakrishna*, New York 1943.
Nityabodhananda, Swami, *The Myths and Symbols in Indian Civilization*, Madras n.d.
Noble, Margaret Elizabeth, *Kali, the Mother*, London 1900.
——, and Ananda K. Coomaraswamy, *Myths of Hinduism*, London 1920.
O'Flaherty, Wendy Doniger, *Asceticism and Eroticism in the Mythology of Śiva*, London 1973.
——, 'The Hindu Symbolism of Cows, Bulls, Stallions and

Mares' in *Art and Archaeology Research Papers*, 8 (1975), pp. 1–7.
——, ed., *Hindu Myths*, Harmondsworth 1975.
O'Malley, L. S. S., *Popular Hinduism*, Cambridge 1935.
Pathak, M. V. S., *History of Śaiva Cults in North India*, Varanasi 1960.
Paynes, Ernest Alexander, *The Śaktas*, Calcutta 1933.
Phillips, Maurice, *The Evolution of Hinduism*, Madras 1903.
Pilai, Tiru G. S., *Introduction and History of Saiva Siddhanta*, Annamalainagar, 1948.
Pinkham, M. W., *Women in the Sacred Scriptures of Hinduism*, New York 1941.
Pusalker, A. D., *Studies in the Epics and Purāṇas of India*, Bombay 1955.
Radhakrishnan, S., *The Hindu View of Life*, London 1927.
——, and Charles A. Moore, *A Source Book in Indian Philosophy*, Princeton 1967.
Raghavan, V., *The Number of Rasas*, Adyar 1940.
——, 'Holy Water' in *Vedanta Kesari*, Madras, November 1940, pp. 243–8.
——, 'Dīpāvali Down the Ages' in *The Hindu*, Madras, November 7, 1961.
Rao, K. B. Ramakrishna, 'The Gunas of Prakṛti According to the Sāṅkhya Philosophy' in *Philosophy East and West*, Vol. 13, April 1963, pp. 61–71.
Ray, Pratap Chandra, trans., *The Mahābhārata*, Calcutta 1890.
Ray Chaudhuri, Anil Kumar, *The Doctrine of Maya*, Calcutta 1950.
Riepe, Dale, *The Naturalistic Tradition in Indian Thought*, Seattle 1961.
Saksena, Shri Krishna, *Nature of Consciousness in Hindu Philosophy*, Benaras 1944.
Salk, Jonas, *Anatomy of Reality: Merging of Intuition and Reason*, New York 1983.
Sarkar, Benoy Kumar, *The Folk Element in Hindu Culture, London* 1917.
Sastri, B. K., *The Bhakti Cult in Ancient India*, Varanasi 1965.
Seal, Brajendranath, *The Positive Sciences of the Ancient Hindus*, London 1915.
Sen, Dinesh Chandra, *Chaitanya and His Age*, Calcutta 1922.
Sharma, T. R., *Studies in the Sectarian Upanisads*, Delhi 1972.
Shastri, Dakshinaranjan, *Origin and Development of the Rituals of Ancestor Worship in India*, Calcutta 1963.
Siegel, L., *Sacred and profane dimensions of love in Indian traditions as exemplified in the Gītagovinda of Jayadeva*, Delhi, n.d.
Singh, Jaideva, *Śiva Sūtras*, Delhi 1979.
——, *Spanda Kārikās*, Delhi 1980.
——, *Vijñānabhairava or Divine Consciousness*, Delhi 1979.
Spratt, P., *Hindu Culture and Personality: A Psychoanalytic Study*, Bombay 1960.
Staal, Frits, *Exploring Mysticism*, Berkeley 1975.
Stevenson, Mrs Sinclair, *The Rites of the Twice-Born: The Religious Quest of India*, London 1920.
Tagore, Rabindranath, *The Religion of Man*, London 1931.
Thite, Ganesh Umakant, *Sacrifice in the Brāhmaṇa-Texts*, Poona, 1975.
Thomas, Edward J., *The Life of Buddha as Legend and History*, New York and London 1927.
Underhill, Muriel M., *The Hindu Religious Year*, London 1921.
Varadachari, M., *Āḻvārs of South India*, Bombay 1966.
Visvanatha Aiyar, S. V., *Racial Synthesis in Hindu Culture*, London 1928.
Vatsyayan, Kapila, *Classical Indian Dance in Literature and the Arts*, New Delhi 1968.
——, *The Square and the Circle of the Indian Arts*, New Delhi 1983.
Walker, Benjamin, *Hindu World*, 2 vols. London 1968.
Weightman, Simon, *Hindiusm in the Village Setting*, Milton Keynes 1978.
Whitehead, Henry, *The Village Gods of South India*, London 1921.
Woodroffe, Sir John, *Shakti and Shākta*, Madras 1929.
Yogeshananda, Swami, *The Vision of Ramakrishna*, Madras, n.d.
Zaehner, Robert Charles, *Hindu and Muslim Mysticism*, London 1960.
——, *Hinduism*, Oxford 1962.
Zimmer, Heinrich, *Myths and Symbols in Indian Art and Civilization*, Bollingen Series VI, Princeton 1946.

GLOSSARY

ABHIŚEKA, ceremonial purification of the deity by bathing, performed at every occasion of worship. Self-purification by bathing.

ĀCĀRA, correct way to perform a ritual.

ĀCHMANA, rite of sipping water from the palm and sprinkling it on the various parts of the body – a symbolic purification. Rite in a series in preparation for the creation of a work of ritual art.

ADHIKĀRA, a disciple's competency to practise spiritual discipline, generally gained through tuition by a guru before initiation.

ADHVAYA, Vedic name, still in use, for the priest who performs the fire sacrifice.

ADITI-UTTĀNAPĀD, the earliest-known Vedic Mother Goddess.

ĀDYĀ-ŚAKTI, the Primal Energy, limitless primordial power. Aspect of the goddess Kālī.

ĀGAMAS, sacred tantric scriptures, regarded as divine revelation, set in the form of dialogues between Śiva and Pārvatī.

AGNI, Vedic fire god, the Sacrifical Fire.

AGNICAYANA, the Vedic fire altar.

AHAṀKĀRA, Ego-consciousness, one of the categories of the Sāṁkhya system (q.v). For the individual *ahaṁkāra* requires to be dissolved in the course of worship.

ĀHNIKA, everyone's daily ritual duties.

AJAPĀ, effortless repetition of a sacred mantra or seed-sound.

ĀKĀŚA, the ether element, one of the five grosser elements making up the universe, whose purification is essential in any ritual worship. Vibration in space, indicating creation, represented by the drum of Śiva.

AKṢAMĀLĀ, string of beads for counting off the names of deities or mantras.

ĀLIPANĀ, name (in Bengal) for an auspicious diagram drawn with rice-paste on a wall or floor. The rite of installation of the deity is often carried out with the icon set on a diagram.

AMBIKĀ, 'Little Mother'. Term for the goddess Durgā.

ĀNANDA, the 'bliss aspect' of Reality, to be experienced through worship. Essential principle of joy, bliss, spiritual ecstasy; the letter ā symbolizing Śakti.

AṆḌA-RŪPA, the concrete form of the deity, represented for worship as the Cosmic Egg.

AṄGANYĀSA, essential rite of worship, the touching of the different parts of the body: heart, head, eyes and navel – a projection of divine entities.

AÑJALI, a gesture with hands joined, palms upward, of offering in worship.

ANTYESHṬI, the funeral rite.

ANUGRAHA, grace of deity, needful for spiritual liberation.

AP, water, one of the five gross elements that make up the universe. The essential purifying element, indispensable for any ritual worship. Each of the elements must be represented and purified in worship; *vymon*, ether; *marut*, air; *tejas*, fire; *kshiti*, earth.

ĀRATĪ, the devotional waving of oil-lamps or other ingredients in front of the deity, an obligatory daily rite.

ARDHANĀRĪŚVARA, the god Śiva and goddess Pārvatī as one deity. Has been frequently represented, but is now infrequently worshipped.

ARGHYA, ritual water; the ritual morning bathe in the river.

ĀSANA, yogic posture, steady posture adopted for meditation or for worship in front of the icon of the deity, yantra diagram etc.

ASURAS, demonic powers, Mahisha-asura, the Buffalo Demon, is the personification of these powers, destroyed when Durgā-pūjā (worship of the goddess Durgā) is performed.

ĀTMAN, the universal substratum of consciousness; the individual self or soul.

ĀTMASAMARPAṆA, attitude of surrender of the self to the chosen deity.

ĀTMAŚUDDHI, self-purification by various processes.

ĀVĀHANĪ-MUDRĀ, inviting (*āvāhana*) or calling upon the deity with a hand-gesture made by holding out both hands together with palms upward, the thumb of each held against the ring finger.

AVATĀRAS, Vishṇu in his ten incarnations, of which Kṛishṇa is the one chiefly worshipped.

AVAYA-MUDRĀ, gesture of the hands giving freedom from fear.

AVIDYĀ, false knowledge or ignorance.

AVYAKTA, the Void, the nonmanifest.

BĀHYAPŪJĀ, external worship of icons etc., as opposed to inner reverence (mānasa-pūjā) and transcendental worship (parā-pūjā).

BALI, sacrifice, gift-offering.

BANDHA, psychic knots, to be dissolved by ritual practices and meditation.

BHAIRAVA and BHAIRAVĪ, Terrible aspects of Śiva and Śakti respectively. Names of rāgas sung at a particular time of year to induce the emotions appropriate to the worship of each of these deity-aspects.

BHAKTI, attitude of fervent devotion to a personal god, as in the worship of Kṛishṇa.

BHĀVA, one's relation to god, chiefly devotion; religious emotion; aesthetic state.

BHOGA, enjoyment or worldly experiences as a 'way' to spiritual liberation.

BHŪTA-SŪDDHI, ritual purification of the five elements (bhūtas): earth, water, fire, air and ether. One of the essential rites in preparation for the making of an icon or other work of ritual art, and for all worship.

BĪJA, seed, as in bīja-mantra, the seed-mantra being the primal sound.

BINDU, point, a metaphysical symbol of the universe in its unmanifested form. A dot symbolizes Śiva. A double dot symbolizes Śiva-Śakti, and is also the *visarga*, a Sanskrit alphabetical sign.

BODHANA, awakening to worship; an essential rite in worship of an icon, and in the making of a work of ritual art.

BODHI, Enlightenment.

BRAHMĀ, as a deity of post-Vedic India, the Creator, and the first god of the Hindu triad.

BRAHMAJÑĀNA, knowledge of Brahman, the Ultimate Reality.

BRAHMAN, Universal Soul, the Absolute, Ultimate Reality.

BRĀHMAṆAS OF BRĀHMINS, first of the four Hindu castes, a priestly sect which conducts the daily rites and sacrifices and studies and teaches the *Vedas* (q.v.).

BRĀHMAṆAS, post-Vedic literature (900–700 BC).

BRAHMĀṆḌA, Cosmic Egg, a symbol of all-pervasive reality.

(ŚRĪ) CAITANYA, noted Hindu saint, born in 1485 at Navadwip, Bengal.

CANDRA, moon, lunar phase.

CHAITANYA, Pure Consciousness. In the practise of internal worship, one considers this to be enshrined within one's body.

CHAKRA, circle; energy-centre in the subtle body. The body's chakras are energized one by one, or in some cases all together simultaneously, in yogic worship.

CHINMAYA RŪPA, transcendental form of the deity.

CIT, Ultimate Reality, Pure Consciousness.

CITTA, the limitation of the Universal Consciousness in the individual mind.

CITTAŚUDHI, purification of the mind.

CITI, Kashmir philosophical concept of power-consciousness; energy of the Absolute that brings about the world-process.

CITŚAKTI, energy of consciousness, the feminine principle.

DARŚANA, visualizing of the deity; 'seeing'; a term applied to all systems of philosophy, meaning that they are divine revelation.

DAŚA MAHĀVIDYĀS, ten tantric goddesses, the 'Transcendental Wisdoms'.

DEVA, god.

DEVATĀ, male or female deity.

DEVATĀŚUDDHI, purification of the image of a deity.

DEVĪ, goddess.

DHARMA, the essential nature or qualities of a thing or individual.

DHYĀNA, deep contemplation, meditation.

DHYĀNA-MUDRĀ, the position of hands, placed one above the other with palms upwards, adopted while in meditation.

DIK, directions of sacred space, to be ritually enclosed.

DĪKṢĀ, initiation or consecration by which spiritual knowledge is imparted.

DĪPA, lighted lamp, moved in a clockwise direction during deity-worship.

DIVĀLĪ, (Sanskrit DIPĀVALĪ), the annual Festival of Lights.

DIVYABHĀVA, the highest plane of feeling.

DRAVYAŚUDDHI, purification of ritual materials.

DURGĀ, the Great Goddess.

DURGĀ-PŪJĀ, worship of the goddess Durgā during her annual festival in autumn.

DVI-JAS, twice-born, born-of-ritual.

GAṆEŚA, elephant-headed god whose consorts are success and good fortune; often invoked at the commencement of ritual worship.

GAṄGĀ, goddess personifying the Ganges River.

GARUḌA, mythical bird, half giant, half eagle. Vehicle of Vishṇu.

GAURIPAṬṬA, the pedestal upon which the Śiva-liṅga is placed within the yoni-shape representing Śakti.

GĀYATRĪ, the most sacred Vedic mantra, personified as the goddess Gāyatrī; the mantra is still widely used today.

GHAṆṬĀS, bell, used in ritual worship.

GHĀṬ, flight of steps leading to the river or temple-tank, where devotions are performed; regarded as the *axis mundi*.

GHAṬA STHĀPANA, ritual establishment of the ceremonial water jar.

GOVINDA, GOVINDA-JI, name of Kṛishṇa.

GRĀMA-DEVATĀS, village deities.

GRANTHI, knot, psychic tangle, obstruction to be overcome in yogic meditation.

GṚIHYA-SŪTRAS, post-Vedic ritual manual concerned with domestic rituals.

GUṆA, attribute, quality, energy of Nature (Prakṛiti). There are three gunas: Sattva (harmony), rajas (motion, activity), and tamas (inertia).

HĀ, sound-symbol of Śakti, divine power.

HAṀSA, goose or swan, the mount of Brahmā. If the word is repeated in inverted form as a mantra: 'so-ham' ('I am He' or 'this am I', it epitomises the whole philosophy of the *Upanishads*.

HANUMĀN, the monkey-god who figures in an episode of the *Rāmāyaṇa*.

HĀVAN, offering or oblation to the Vedic sacrificial fire.

HIRAṆYA-GARBHA, Golden Womb; Cosmic Egg floating on the primeval waters.

HLĀDINĪ, blissful Śakti (energy) of the Supreme Being. According to Vaisṇavites (followers of Vishṇu), Rādhā is the hlādinī-śakti of Kṛishṇa (the most important avatāra of Vishṇu).

HOMA, the Vedic fire ritual.

HOMA-KUṆḌA, a fire altar hollowed out of the ground.

INDRĀGNI, deity combining the Vedic gods Indra and Agni.

INDRIYAS, the ten faculties of sensation and perception in the human body, to be controlled by spiritual discipline.

ISHṬA-DEVATĀ, ISHṬA-DEVĪ, an individual's chosen deity.

JAḌAŚAKTI, the material cause of creation.

JAGAT, the dynamic (ever-moving) world-process.

JAPA, repetition of a mantra.

JAPAMĀLĀ, necklace for the counting of mantras.

JALAŚUDDHI, purification of water.

JĪVA, JIVĀTMĀ, individual soul.

JIVAN-MUKTA, one who is liberated in this life.

JYOTI, spiritual light.

KĀLA, Time, the power that conditions or limits the existence of unchangeable elements in matter.

KALĀ, an aspect of the Great Mother. Also denotes Prakṛiti (Nature), Śakti (Energy) or Māyā (Veiling Power).

KĀLĪ, the Divine Śakti (Energy), the goddess representing the creative and destructive aspects of nature.

KALKI, future and final avatāra (incarnation) of Vishṇu.

KALPA, aeon; a 'day' of Brahmā the Creator.

KĀMA, enjoyment, desire as cosmic power.

KAMALĀ, lotus, name of the goddess Lakshmī.

KĀMYA, 'optional' rites, as against obligatory rites (*nitya*).

KANYĀ-KUMĀRI, 'young virgin' – name of the temple for worship of the Goddess at Cape Comorin, South India.

KĀRAṆA, cause, source; in tantric chakra-pūjā (worship in a circle), ritual of wine.

KĀRAṆA-DEHA, KĀRAṆA-ŚARIRA, subtle body, the purified body.

KARANYĀSA, ritual of 'feeling' the deity; the fingers are used to touch the body with the pronunciation of seed-sounds to invoke deities.

KAULA, 'left-hand' sect of tantrism, in which rites of symbolic union are practised with a female partner who becomes Śakti for the purpose of the ritual.

KĀYOTSARGA, body liberation, release from the bondage of the gross body.

KOLAM, name in Tamil Nadu, and generally in South India, for an auspicious diagram made with rice-paste on a wall or floor.

KOṢA, KUṢI, ceremonial water stoups symbolizing the male and female principles respectively. Water is kept in the kuṣi until taken out by the koṣa during ritual worship.

KṚISHṆA, lampblack, used for making ritual images.

KRIYĀ, action, ritual performance.

KSHITI, earth, one of the five gross elements that make up the universe, to be purified in ritual worship, as also *vymon*, ether; *marut*, air; *tejas*, fire; *ap*, water.

KULA, clan or family membership determining the kind of ritual used.

KUMĀRĪ-PŪJĀ, rites of virgin-worship.

KUṆḌA, fire altar.

KUṆḌALINĪ, dormant psychic power, lying coiled like a sleeping serpent at the base of the spine, in the energy-centre known as the mūlādhāra chakra. To be awakened to ascend through successive chakras (q.v.) with ritual and meditation.

LAKSHMĪ, goddess of wealth, good fortune, beauty, fertility.

LATĀ, the female partner of the aspirant.

LAYA, total dissolution; energy cross-points acting as absorption or dissolution points.

LAYAYOGA, the higher form of Haṭhayoga, the awakening of Kuṇḍalinī (q.v.)

LĪLĀ, divine play, which brings the universe into being.

LIṄGA, symbol of Śiva, generative force in its pre-evolutionary aspect.

LIṄGA-ŚARĪRA, totality of the subtle or psychic body.

LOKA, plane of existence.

MADHUPARKA, mixture of honey and milk to be offered during rituals.

MAHĀMĀI, Great Mother.

MĀNAT, pledge or vow, offered to a deity when a boon is sought.

MANASĀ, serpent goddess.

MĀNASA-PŪJĀ, inner or 'mental' worship.

MAṆḌALA, circle; a mystic diagram of squares and circles, symbolic of cosmic forces, used as a support for concentration.

MAṄGALA-GHAṬA, consecrated water pot.

MANTRA, sacred syllable, formula based on the principle that sound has spiritual significance and power.

MANTRA-ŚAKTI, power of the mantra.

MĀRGA, path, way, means to spiritual liberation.

MARUT, air, one of the five gross elements that make up the universe, which must be purified in ritual, as also *vymon*, ether; *tejas*, fire; *ap*, water; *kshiti*, earth.

MĀTṚIKĀ, Divine Mother; power of the letter or word; base of all knowledge.

MĀYĀ, false knowledge; manifestation of apparently separate entities; veiling power.

MOHA, delusion by sensuous desire.

MOKṢA, salvation, liberation.

MUDRĀ, (*mud*=joy; *rā*=to give), positions of the hands which when employed in yogic practice induces the bliss of spiritual consciousness.

MUHŪRTA, the critical moment for the performance of a rite.
MUKTI, final liberation from the wheel of life and bondage of existence.
MŪRTI, manifest form or image of the deity.
NĀDA, vibrational energy, manifesting as sound; primal and cosmic sound.
NĀDA-BINDU, primal vibration, the seed-sound out of which the universe emanates.
NĀDA-BRAHMAN, Pure Consciousness in the form of cosmic sound-vibration.
NĀḌĪ, psychic channels in the physical body; subtle nerves of the human body.
NAKṢATRAS, lunar mansions.
NĀRĀYAṆA, Universal Consciousness, symbolized by the Śālagrāma, a natural river-rounded stone.
NIRVIKALPA-SAMĀDHI, the bliss-state in which the distinction of the knower, knowledge and known vanishes.
NITYAPŪJĀ, obligatory daily rites, worship.
NIYATI, fate or destiny; limitation by cause and effect.
NYĀSA, projection of divine entities into various parts of the body by means of mantras and touching of the part.
PĀDA, step, footprint, as in Vishṇu-pāda, the footprint of Vishṇu, symbolically containing all that makes up the world.
PADMA, lotus, symbol of transformation, purity, fertility.
PADMĀ, a name of the goddess Lakshmī.
PAÑCHABUHŪTAS, five gross elements, namely, earth, water, fire, air and space or ether, which must be purified in ritual.
PAÑCHA-PRADĪPAS, ritual lamps, generally with five (*pañcha*) wicks.
PAÑCHAPACĀRA, five ingredients used for worship; *gaṇdha* (perfumed substances), *puṣpa* (flowers), *dhūpa* (incense), *dīpa* (lamp-flame) and *naivedya* (food-offerings).
PAÑCHĀYATANA, rite of invocation of five deities.
PARA, the highest stage of consciousness.
PARAM, the Supreme.
PARAMA ŚIVĀ, the Highest Reality.
PARĀ-PRAKṚITI, transcendental Nature.
PARĀ-PŪJĀ, the highest form of worship, transcendental worship.
PARĀ-RŪPA, the supreme form of the deity, as against the *sthula* (gross) form and *sukṣma* (subtle) form.
PARĀ-ŚAKTI, the energy of the Supreme Being, as cause and instrument of creation.
PĀRTHANĀ, prayer, supplication.
PĀRVATĪ, goddess, consort of Śiva.
PATUĀS, folk artists making paintings and other ritual objects (as at Kalighat Temple, south Calcutta).
PIṆḌA, the individual body, the gross body.
PĪTA, yellow pigment used for colouring ritual images.
PĪṬHA, holy places of Śakti, traditionally 51 or 108 in number.
PRADAKṢINA, clockwise circumambulation.
PRAJĀPATI, the Vedic 'Lord of Creation'.
PRAKṚITI, counterpart of the male principle Purusha; creative energy; the source of objectivity, cosmic substance; the primal female, or Nature.
PRALAYA, dissolution of a cycle of aeons or *yugas* (q.v.).
PRĀṆA-PRAṬISTHĀ, breathing of deity into image.
PRASĀDA, rite of offering food.
PṚTHIVI, earth principle.
PŪJĀ, ritual worship.
PURĀṆAS, Hindu post-Vedic verse-dialogue scriptures (4th–16th centuries), expounding in legendary form the powers and deeds of gods and goddesses.
PŪRNĀBHIṢEKA, the highest form of initiation, provided only by a guru.
PŪRṆA-GHAṬA, consecrated water pot.
PURUSHA, Pure Consciousness; the male principle, counterpart of Prakṛiti or Nature, the female principle.
PUSHPAPĀTRAS, copper ritual offering-plates.
PUSHPĀÑJALI, handful of flowers offered to the deity during ritual worship.
RĀDHĀ, chief of the gopīs or cow-maidens, favourite consort of the god Kṛishṇa.
RĀGA, veiling power of attachment.
RAJAS, principle of motion, a constituent of Prakṛiti or Nature. Female seed, menstrual flow.
RAKTA, red pigment used for the colouring of ritual images.
RĀMA, avatāra of Vishṇu, hero of the *Rāmāyaṇa*.
RAṄGOLI, name in Maharashtra for auspicious diagram drawn with rice-paste on the wall or floor.
RASA, essence of a thing; aesthetic delight; pleasure.
RĀSALĪLĀ, circular (maṇḍala) dance, with Kṛishṇa dancing at the centre of a ring of adoring gopīs (cow-maidens).
RIṢHI, inspired seer, sage.
ŚABDA-BRAHMA, Brahma or Brahman, the Absolute, as the primal sound-energy.
ṢAḌAṄGANYĀSA, projection by touch and sound of divine entities into six parts of the body – heart, forehead, crown of the head, arm, eyes and navel region.
SĀDHAKA, seeker, spiritual aspirant.
SĀDHANĀ, progressive spiritual discipline, or quest.
SĀDHU, holy man.
SAGUṆA, defined, with attributes.
ŚAKTI, kinetic aspect of the Ultimate Principle, conceived as the feminine principle through which the manifestation of the universe is effected. The important modes of this energy are *cit* (intelligence), *ānanda* (bliss), *icchā* (will), *jñāna* (knowledge) and *kriyā* (action).

ŚAKTI-PĀTA, descent of Śakti to bless.

ŚĀLAGRĀMA, symbol of Vishṇu's essence, and of that of his consort Lakshmī.

SAMĀDHI, deep meditation.

SAMARASA, undifferentiated essence.

SAMARPAṆA, dedication of ritual objects, a rite in the preparation of a work of ritual art.

SAṀHITĀS, post-Vedic ritual manual, concerned with domestic observances.

SAṀKHYA, major system of philosophy founded by the sage Kapila, *c.*500 BC.

SAṄDHYĀ, ritual worship at dawn and in the evening twilight.

SAṄKALPA, resolution; one of the first rites involved in the making of a work of ritual art and in deity-worship.

SANNYĀSI, renunciate.

SAT, represents the Supreme as it is, Pure Existence.

SATCITĀNANDA, existence, consciousness and bliss, as a unity.

SATTVA, the highest of the guṇas (q.v.), principle of equilibrium, truth, intelligence-stuff.

SAUCHA, bodily purity.

SHĀSTRAS, sacred books, scriptures of divine authority.

ŚILPI-YOGIN, maker of ritual art.

SINDŪRA, vermilion powder-pigment used in worship.

ŚIṢYA, disciple.

SĪTĀ, wife of Rāma, in the legends of the *Rāmāyaṇa*.

ŚIVA, Pure Consciousness, transcendent divine principle; the Destroyer; third god of the Hindu triad, the first being Brahmā the Creator, the second Vishṇu the Preserver.

SLOKA, Sanskrit stanza or verse in general.

ŚODHANA, purification.

SOMA, an intoxicating drink known in Vedic times.

SPANDA, throb or vibration in the Void, initiating creation.

SPARŚA-DĪKṢĀ, initiation by touch.

ŚRĪ YANTRA, the most celebrated power diagram, a pictorial, symbolic pattern of the cosmic field in creation.

SṚISHṬI, creation.

STHĀNA ŚUDDHI, purification of the place of worship.

ŚUNYA, a state in which there is no distinct consciousness of knower and known.

SŪRYA, the sun god.

SŪRYA NAMASKĀRA, salutation to the sun at sunrise.

SVĀHĀ, the terminal sound of a number of mantras.

SVARŪPA, essential nature of a deity.

SVASTI-VACHANA, invoking blessings, benediction at the commencement of a solemn observance or rite.

SVETA, white pigment used in making ritual images.

TAMAS, power of inertia, the lowest of the three guṇas (q.v.), *sattva*, *rajas* and *tamas*, that make up Prakṛiti, Nature or the Ground.

TANMĀTRA, infra-atomic or subtle energy potential.

TAPAS, heat, creative fervour.

TARPAṆA, offering of water to deities, or to deceased ancestors.

TATTVA, 'thatness', the very being of a thing.

TEJAS, fire, one of the five grosser elements making up the universe, to be purified in ritual worship, as also *vymon*, ether; *marut*, air; *ap*; water.

TILAKA or TĪKĀ, a distinctive ritual mark on the forehead, designating one's sect.

TĪRTHA, pilgrimage centre; literally, river bathing-place or ford.

TRIMŪRTI, Three Forms.

TRISŪLA, trident of Śiva, representing creation, preservation, dissolution.

TRUṬI, atomic point of time. Unit in 'ritual' time.

UMĀ, daughter of the Himalayas; goddess-consort of Śiva; the goddess Pārvatī.

UPĀCĀRA, the series of rites performed before an installed deity.

UPANANYANA, pupilage and 'second birth' of a twice-born boy.

UPANISHADS, spiritual doctrines, ancient Indian philosophic writings composed in their present form during the period *c.* 1000 to 800 BC. The fundamental concept of the *Upanishads* is the identity of the individual soul with the Universal Soul. They are essentially an inquiry into the nature of Ultimate Reality.

UPĀSANĀ, ritual worship.

USHĀ, goddess, the Vedic Dawn.

VĀMA MĀRGA, 'left-hand' path, tantric practices which use as ingredients of worship the five 'm's: *madya*, wine; *māmsa*, meat; *matsya*, fish; *mūdrā*, parched cereal, and *maithuna*, sexual union.

VARA-MUDRĀ, hand-gesture granting boons.

VARṆA, Sanskrit letter, used in worship.

VARṆĀŚRAMA, traditional code of ritual due to self and to society at large.

VASTRA-HARAṆ, episode of the stealing of the gopīs' (cow-maidens') clothes by Kṛishṇa.

VĀYU, vital air; breath control.

VEDAS, original religious source-books of India. Revealed knowledge of the Aryans, consisting of 100,000 verses in four divisions, the *Ṛig Veda* (*c.* 2000–1500 BC), the earliest literature of the world; the *Yajur Veda*; the *Sāma Veda*; the *Atharva Veda*.

VIBHŪTI, supernatural powers of gurus or Enlightened souls.

VISARGA, double dot (double bindu), symbolizing Śiva-Śakti; also a Sanskrit alphabetical sign.

VISARJANA, rite of bidding farewell. At the close of customary worship the image of the deity is immersed, either actually or symbolically. After festival worship, the temporary image of the deity will be carried to the nearest temple-tank or river to be thrown into the water.

VISHṆU, the second god of the Hindu triad, the Preserver, just as Brahmā is the Creator and Śiva the Destroyer.
VISHṆU-PĀDA, footprint of Vishṇu, containing all that is.
VIŚVARŪPA, Cosmic Form, Kṛishṇa as the universe.
VRATAS, traditional rites of goddess-worship, generally performed by women and girls.
VYMON, ether, one of the five gross elements that make up the universe, which must be purified in worship, as also *marut*, air; *tejas*, fire; *ap*, water; *kshiti*, earth.
YAJMĀNA, Vedic name for the priest of the fire sacrifice, still in use in Kerala.
YAJÑA, Vedic fire altar, the fire sacrifice.
YANTRA, form-symbol of a deity; aid to contemplation; generally a diagram or geometrical representation, suggesting by its form-relationships the characteristics of the deity.
YOGA, union; a path on which the individual self is united with the Universal Self.
YOGI, one who seeks to attain essential identity with Reality.
YOGINI, female yogi; goddesses, generally sixty-four in number.
YONI, the matrix of generation, womb; a symbol of cosmic mysteries; the primal root of the source of objectivization. Downward-pointing triangle symbolizing the yoni, the female sex organ.
YUGAS, cosmic ages, aeons. The four yugas are Satya or Kṛita-yuga, Tretā-yuga, Dvāpara-yuga and Kali-yuga, the present age of mankind. This began at midnight between 17 and 18 February 3102 BC, and has still almost 427,000 years to run before it is brought to an end, when Vishṇu will appear in the form of Kalki and destroy the world. It will then re-enter its original state, and be created again.

Plate acknowledgments

Photograph Ahmed Ali, Calcutta, 33; photographs Archaeological Survey of India, New Delhi, 110, 124; Asutosh Museum, Calcutta University, 38, 70, 126; collection C.L. Bharany, New Delhi, 67, 86–95, 103; collection Bharat Kala Bhavan, Banaras, 1; Chandigarh Museum (photograph Archaeological Survey of India) 111; photograph Bala Chowdhury, London, 52; J.C. Ciancimino 3, 4, 15, 65 (photograph Allyson P. Kneib, San Diego), 106; Cleveland Museum of Art: gift of Mr and Mrs Severance A. Millikin 18, purchase from the J.H. Wade Fund 104, Mr and Mrs William E. Ward collection 75; photograph Dakshineswar Temple, Calcutta, 99; Collection Villiers David, London, 66, 100; photograph S.C. Duggal, New Delhi, 101; Galley 43, London, 107; photographs courtesy Government of India Tourist Office, London, 21, 53; photograph Parvati Hamilton, London, 54; photograph Robin Hamilton, London, 26; India Office Library, London, 31, 68; Indian Museum, Calcutta (photographs Archaeological Survey of India) 37, 108; photographs Madhu Khanna 17, 32, 41, 46–8, 55, 59, 64, 76, 78–9; collection Martha Longenecker, San Diego (photographs Allyson P. Kneib) 19–20, 24; photographs Isamu Maruyama, Tokyo, 22–3, 51, 113; collection Jagdish Mittal, Hyderabad, 25; Ajit Mookerjee collection 5–11, 29, 69, 105, 121, 125, figs pp. 50, 64, 92; photographs Priya Mookerjee, 16, 30, 39, 42, 50, 56–7, 60–63, 69–74, 81–5, 112, 114–16, 118–19; collection Dr Maurie D. Pressman, Clearwater, 102 (photograph Allyson P. Kneib, San Diego); Naprstek Museum, Prague, 80; National Museum, New Delhi, 28, 122; photograph Lennart Nilsson, Stockholm, 2; photograph Jean-Louis Nou 127; private collection 97; collection Robert Ravicz, Los Angeles, 123 (photograph Allyson P. Kneib, San Diego) 123; photograph the late Mrs Ruth Reeves 108; photograph courtesy Arturo Schwarz, Milan, 58; photographs Mangla Sharda 40, 44–5, 49; Srinagar Museum, Kashmir (photograph Dr Maurie D. Pressman) 109; photographs courtesy Professor Frits Staal, University of California, 12–14, 34–5; photographs J. Swaminathan, New Delhi, 27, (Chandigarh Museum) 36, 43; photograph courtesy David Tremayne, London, 117; photograph courtesy Vedanta Society of California, Hollywood, 98; collection Jan Wichers, Hamburg, 77, 96.

INDEX

Numbers in italics refer to Notes on Plates

Index